How to Write Your Life Stories is outstanding because it *shows* rather than *tells* how to write the stories of your life—and does so with clarity, wisdom, and humor.
—Lucy G. Saroyan, writer

If you can't join Steve Boga's writing class, the next best thing is reading his book, *How to Write Your Life Stories*. He presents an organized, effective recipe for overcoming that familiar complaint: "My life hasn't been eventful enough to write about."
—Jim Fitch, author of *Desert Sailor*

How to Write Your Life Stories is an easy-to-read, how-to-write book. It belongs on your bookshelf next to the dictionary and thesaurus.
—Chuck Kensler, memoirist

Anyone can write a memoir, but if you want to write one that people want to read, you need Steve Boga's help. His book is a full-service guide, full of practical tips and exercises to help you hone your literary skills. And he makes you laugh! This book is a treasure.
—Rosemary Manchester, host of "A Novel Idea," on KRCB radio

How to Write Your Life Stories

Memoirs That People Want to Read

Steve Boga

Cover photograph: Madeleine Boga

Cover design: Karen Boga

This book was printed in the United States of America.

To order additional copies of this book, go to
memoirwritings.com or
email lifestories@memoirwritings.com.
59216

To my Friday writers, for their stories and the courage to tell them.

Contents

BEFORE YOU BEGIN

STARTING YOUR LIFE STORIES

KEEPING MOMENTUM

PUBLISHING YOUR LIFE STORIES

APPENDICES

SOME MEMOIRS

RESOURCES

Preface

Although I performed capably in English classes, I was eight years out of college before I began to see writing as having a purpose other than informing my parents I was alive and well in Kabul or Katmandu.

Then one day in 1977, camping near Florence, Italy, I was moved by an inexplicable urge to relate an experience I'd had three years earlier in Meshad, Iran. Two Iranian merchants had plied my friend Tim and me with lunch and adulterated tea, showed us about a hundred rugs, and sold us two of them. This was a story that had to be told, or so I thought.

I bought a notebook and planted myself in the stands of an abandoned soccer stadium, and wrote. It was harder than I thought, but after five hours I had a 1,500-word rough draft. A week later I had a 1,000-word third draft. It didn't occur to me that I was writing a memoir.

As I continued to travel, I fictionalized my memoirs and kept writing. When I returned home to California, I converted an alcove into a work area. And I wrote, completing a novel two years later. The Meshad story, which launched it all, was eventually dropped as irrelevant.

When the local teachers went on strike and I could no longer substitute teach without being tagged a scab, I stayed home and wrote.

After three years I had completed (a dicey word for any writer) a long nonfiction piece, *Dress Blues and Tennis Shoes*, about my travels through the South umpiring professional baseball with a black partner. Although I didn't call it that, it was a memoir.

I signed with an agent who agreed to try to sell both manuscripts. He eventually failed, but it wasn't his fault. Maybe the public wasn't ready for my work, but my work definitely wasn't ready for the public. Although I couldn't see that truth, I kept writing and got better and eventually my creations found publishers.

I've learned a lesson or two along the way, but here's the most important one: It's the writing that counts. Doing work we love is what enriches our lives. Wealth and fame may come to a few, but it is the joy of work, the quiet exultation we feel after crafting a winning metaphor or a gripping lead that keeps the writer coming back for more.

Introduction

*A writer is rarely so well inspired
as when he talks about himself.*

–Anatole France

Each of us is a link in a generational chain. And each of us has a story to tell that is as unique as our fingerprints. Back in tribal days, we could count on storytellers to pass along ancestral wisdom, values, and traditions. In Western societies, sociologists record our history, but the substance and vitality of our lives is lost to our descendants. It's left to us to tell the personal stories.

In this age of scattered families, writing down your personal stories is a way for future generations to truly know your life and times. By reading your memoirs, they will become intimate with your culture; they will come to understand your work, lifestyle, travel, values, and beliefs; and they will get to know the people you loved and lost. If your stories are well written, they will be fascinated by what you have to say.

Many people decline to write their memoirs because their stories seem dull, uneventful. But if your life has known goals and obstacles, conflict and emotion, you have the makings of a gripping story. Others decline because they see it as an overwhelming task. In this book you will see it's not overwhelming. You will learn how much easier it is when you take it chapter by chapter, one story at a time.

What is Memoir?

Memoirs are written memories clustered around a theme, a piece of your life told in detail. The theme may be travel, life on a farm, a career, a city, the theater, any aspect of life. Memoirs tell of particular times or episodes. They are not narratives of a long life history, for that is autobiography. Instead, they

13

are selected parts: the trips, the jobs, the people. A memoir can be as long as a page, a chapter, or a book.

Memoirs might have titles such as: "My Cowboy Year," "My Summer in Madrid," "Our Depression Family," "Selling Door-to-Door," "The World's Fair," "On the Road with My Trombone," "Pilot of a P-47, "Home Again."

Writers of memoirs use the first person, the "I," to relate and link selected stories of their own past, to tug the reader, and to show what it was like as a Nebraska sodbuster, an early airmail pilot, an inner-city social worker. A retired actor might write about what happened backstage, a foster mother about her disabled child, a grandfather about war experiences he could neither forget nor duplicate.

Memoirs can stand alone or be linked into a series to show portraits of your life. They are glimpses into the past, to another time and place: a war, a career, a vacation, a love affair. They are memories of the events that are most vivid.

It may be all the rage for celebrities to reveal intimate parts of their lives, but memoirs have value for ordinary people leading ordinary lives. Readers in the next century will lead lives far different and will look back in wonder. For that matter, today's writers are full of their own wonder—that they are here in the 21st century, that so much has happened to them and their world while they lived in it.

William Zinsser says in his classic book *On Writing Well* that memoir is the art of inventing the truth. By "art" he means that writers have taught themselves, as tellers of tales, how to be effective in the telling. It's a reminder that writing is a craft to be learned. The goal: to find the best way to put down on paper the remembrances of the past and the people who were part of it.

Determine early who your audience is, whom you are writing for. Are you writing for your own satisfaction? Your children? A writing group? As you choose what to include and what to keep out, hold your audience foremost in your mind. The content, form, and style of your story depend on your purpose.

Simplicity and clarity are the first goals as you learn the craft of assembling the pieces of your life into an artful and truthful whole.

Be specific, not general. Focus on the details of a particular incident anchored in a specific time and place. Writer Anne Lamott advises us to write down only as much as we can see through a one-inch picture frame. In other words, don't try to do too much too fast.

Why Write Memoir?

I've become a big fan of the memoir. Over the years I've read and listened to thousands of life stories written by hundreds of men and women. I've seen the benefits reaped, and they have nothing to do with getting published.

- *It's stimulating.* Research shows that engaging in stimulating activities slows mental aging. Mental exercise can help your brain function at a higher level than it would otherwise. If thirty minutes on the treadmill each day is good for your body, imagine how the brain benefits from thirty or more minutes a day wrestling with your life stories.

- *It's healing.* Teaching memoir has taught me there's no statute of limitations on emotion. I've seen octogenarians weep over childhood events. By working through the pain of life, writers can find understanding and comfort.

- *It's creative.* Creativity is the route to self discovery and authenticity. As you create, you plumb the depths of your being, accessing what you think and believe. You may be surprised by what you discover.

- *It's connective.* Writing your stories will help you reconnect with people, family and friends, living and dead.

- *It's educational.* As William Zinsser says, memories are a powerful search mechanism. You will learn things about yourself, your family, and the world.

- *It's purposeful.* Many retirees confront a serious psychological problem: a lack of purpose. Writing about your past life gives your present life meaning.

- *It's gratifying.* You will swell with pride each time you finish a life story.

- *It's liberating.* Get past the notion that writing about yourself is egotistical. Give yourself permission to tell us who you really are. Once you do that, limitations fall away. Find your voice and feel the freedom in that.

- *It improves recall.* Studies show that improving our ability to process language tends to improve our recall.

- *It preserves memories.* If not written down, those memories die with their owners.

- *It's a gift.* Naomi, a student of mine, decided at age 90 to profile her family and friends, a tribute to their lives. When she finished, she said with satisfaction, "Now that's what I wanted to do. It's like leaving a gift for my family."

- *It's fun.*

Why Write Well?

You may have led a fascinating life, but if you don't become a good storyteller, no one will read about it. Three of my memoir students were sailors at Pearl Harbor on December 7, 1941, and two of them made it sound, well, ordinary. They preferred to write about ships rather than sailors, guns rather than gunners. On the other hand, someone with a more mundane life but polished writing skills can infuse seemingly ordinary events with meaning. One of my students, Georgia Fowler, did just that when she recounted a simple childhood moment.

Georgia's grandfather, building a fence, asks her to run to the hardware store and get some ten penny nails. The reader is right along with that little girl as she skips toward the store. We're right there when panic hits: She doesn't have the ten pennies. But lo! She can charge it to Grandpa's account. After taking the nails to Grandpa, she slips out and runs down to the ice cream shop. We hear the bell tinkle as she opens the door. We feel her bubbling excitement as Mr. Brody digs out three scoops—vanilla, chocolate, strawberry—and places them on a cone. And we feel her disappointment when he takes the cone back, because Grandpa has no charge account at the sweet shop. In the end, little Georgia is sitting in Grandpa's lap, getting a remedial lesson in the credit system. The story is told with emotion, dialogue, a touch of humor, and a heap of humanity.

Georgia's story is my answer to those who say, "I can't write my memoirs—I've lived a boring life." After all, everyone has had an ice-cream-shop moment.

The skill lies in unlocking your mental vault, then telling the tale well enough to grip someone other than Mom.

In Sum

"Write what you know," we are told. In other words, don't write about Paris high fashion unless you have been there and seen it from the inside;

don't write about the sins of the Hollywood film industry unless you know that world well.

Therein lies the beauty of memoir. You are tackling a subject you know better than anyone else on earth. Even if thousands of others were alongside you at Pearl Harbor or the Obama inauguration, yours is a unique viewpoint. No one else saw that day—or any other day—as you did. No one else can tell your story.

Can you feel the power in that?

memoirwritings.com

BEFORE YOU BEGIN

Chapter 1

Love to Write

Writing is the only thing that, when I do it,
I don't feel I should be doing something else.

—Gloria Steinem

Years ago, when I was profiling dozens of world-class climbers, cyclists, and runners for magazine articles and books, people frequently asked me what the athletes had in common. My answer was always the same: "They love what they do." Although they have superior skills, it is their joy, their passion for their sport that makes them great.

That, first and foremost, is what you need to bring to the writing game.

Best-selling author Anne Lamott knows what's important: "You'll find yourself at work on, maybe really into, another book, and once again you figure out that the real payoff is the writing itself, that a day when you've gotten your work done is a good day, that total dedication is the point."

Do you feel like that after a good day at the desk? Something close? Writing is hard enough that if you don't love it, if you would rather *be* a writer than *do* the writing, you should reconsider this avocation.

On the other hand, maybe you feel something akin to the love for writing revealed here by author Dorothy West: "When I was seven, I said to my mother, may I close the door? And she said, yes, but why do you want to close the door? And I said because I want to think. And when I was eleven, I said to my mother, may I lock the door? And she said yes, but why do you want to lock your door? And I said because I want to write."

[See Appendix A, Love to Write]

Chapter 2

Learn the Basics of Good Writing

I try to leave out the parts that people skip.

—Elmore Leonard

Whether your focus is memoir, essay, fiction, or journalism, the basics of good writing remain the same.

Good writing is aimed at a specific audience. The writer knows the audience and tailors the work to establish a kinship with her readers. The audience understands her even if they don't always agree with her.

Good writing is interesting. The writer draws the reader in by his choice of words and ideas, by his ability to tell a ripping good yarn. He holds the reader's attention from beginning to end.

Good writing is simple and concise. The prose is tight, and ideas are expressed clearly. The writer, through diligent editing, has eliminated all unnecessary words, sentences, and paragraphs.

Good writing reflects the clear thinking of the author. Poor writing is often the product of murky thinking. A good writer knows what she wants to say, and has examined—and reexamined—the content and organization of her material to make sure she has said it.

Good writing is fresh. The writing flows smoothly, seamlessly, free of redundancies and clichés.

Good writing relies on strong imagery. Good writers paint pictures. Descriptions are precise and colorful, stimulating the senses and transporting the reader to the scene the writer has created.

Good writing features correct grammar, spelling, word usage, and punctuation.

Chapter 3

Resolve to Write Regularly

Writing is easy: All you do is sit staring at a blank sheet of paper until drops of blood form on your forehead.

—Gene Fowler

Somerset Maugham worked 4 hours a day; Aldous Huxley 5 hours; Ernest Hemingway 6 hours; Flaubert 7 hours, Joseph Conrad 8 hours. Stephen King once claimed he worked 363 days a year, taking off only Christmas and his birthday; later he admitted he'd fibbed—he actually worked every day of the year.

But take heart: You can be a writer without making that level of commitment. Aim to write daily; settle for no less than twice a week. If you find you've gone weeks without writing, warning bells should sound. Either they will spur you to sit and write, or not. If so, kudos; if not, time to find a new hobby.

If you decide to stick with it, give yourself every chance to succeed. Develop a routine. In fact, the routine is more important than the production. Even no production is okay. As novelist James Jones advised, "Force yourself to sit four hours at the table. Sometimes you get nothing, but the self-discipline is good for you. Somewhere inside you'll be working."

When I'm sitting at my desk staring out the window, my wife doesn't realize I'm working.

—Herb Caen

23

Chapter 4

Create a Workspace

If I fall asleep with a pen in my hand, don't remove it—
I might be writing in my dreams.

—Danzae Pace

I once lived in a converted water tower surrounded by 200-foot-high redwood trees. One day a visitor, awed by the serene beauty of the place, remarked, "Anyone could write here!" That's the kind of space you're looking for: your personal paradise. Find a place that makes you feel both comfortable and inspired, a sanctuary. For most, that means a private desk, ideally in your own room or office, from which you can banish intruders. For almost everyone, it means peace and quiet.

Keep in mind, however, that there are no hard-and-fast rules. Hemingway wrote in crowded Parisian cafes. Others have written standing up, in bed, even in bathtubs. Find an environment that encourages you to work.

One drawback of working at home is that distractions lurk everywhere. It's easy to be diverted by the *New York Times* crossword puzzle, the sports section, or that vacuum cleaner that needs fixing.

Here's how one writer described a morning's struggle with word count: "In order not to write, I cleaned a chainsaw, tried to train some vines up a trellis, rearranged a stack of boards in the basement, pondered making a goat harness for a friend, read the last issue of *Popular Mechanics*, and sawed four old iron-fence palings into a dozen 12-inch rods for petunia boxes."

Chapter 5

Make Time to Write

It takes a good deal of experience to become natural.

—Willa Cather

"How do I find time to write?"—it's the beginner's lament. Granted, writing, if done properly, is hard work and even professional writers have to overcome excuses for not being on the job.

The two most common reasons people don't write:

- You don't love it. You love the idea of being a writer more than doing the writing. Eventually, you will drift to something else—painting, lumberjacking—and for a time that will seem equally romantic. If you find yourself going for weeks without writing, you should question your love for the craft.

- Life gets in the way. Maybe it's family or work or other people that lures you from the desk. You love writing, but "where did the week go?" You, my friend, need to develop a schedule.

What schedule you adopt is completely up to you. There are dawn writers, daylight writers, and dusk writers. But all of them, a few lapses aside, stick to a schedule.

Develop a Writing Schedule

Don't make the mistake of thinking you'll write when you feel inspired, when your muse slaps you upside the head. Thomas Edison said that genius

25

is 1 percent inspiration and 99 percent perspiration, and that applies to no pursuit more than writing.

Find your best time to write. Leon Uris was a twilight writer. Are you sharpest in the morning or at night? For me, no contest—I'm a morning person who can't write my name after ten at night. I love working mornings when it's dark and quiet, and others in my time zone are asleep. What about your biorhythms? Be honest with yourself and schedule accordingly.

As Dominick Dunne advises, "Set a certain time each day to be your writing time, and nothing—nothing—must interfere with that time. THAT IS YOUR WRITING TIME, in capital letters."

How to Find 30 Minutes a Day

- Get up thirty minutes early and write before others arise.

- Stay up a half-hour later than usual.

- If you work in an office, eat at your desk and write.

- Stop at the library for thirty minutes on your way home from work.

- Write on the commuter train, bus, or ferry.

- Ask your partner to take care of the kids for a half-hour.

- If you have school-age children, postpone your chores for thirty minutes after they leave for school.

- Manage your time more efficiently. Pay attention to where your discretionary time goes and cut thirty minutes of waste.

- If you still find yourself saying, "I don't have time for writing," ask yourself what you mean by that. Do you need to manage your time more wisely? Or is writing not as important to you as you thought?

Exercise

Make writing a habit, like eating.

[See Appendix B, Make Time to Write]

Chapter 6

Become More Observant

*On the outskirts of every agony sits
some observant fellow who points.*

—Virginia Woolf

As we age, we learn to block out stimuli that might deter or divert us from getting from point A to point B. Though that attitude makes us more efficient, it also means we stop noticing the "little things."

To write at your creative best, you'll need to readjust your mindset and begin allowing your brain to acknowledge and register the details you've been blocking out. It may seem difficult at first, but with practice, a whole new world of inspiration will reveal itself.

Here are some activities to get you started:

Listen

Sit quietly for five minutes a day. Don't talk, don't move; just listen. Force yourself to hear—really hear—the world around you. Become aware of the sounds you ordinarily ignore, like your neighbor's wind chimes or the low hum of your refrigerator. You'll be amazed at all the noises you've been missing.

Observe

Go to a park, a concert, a mall, wherever you can watch people. Or head for the hills to observe flora and fauna. Record what you see, smell, and hear.

Move

Boost your observation skills through movement. Walk around a neighborhood or hike a trail—breathe deeply. Force your heart and muscles to work harder than usual and you'll wind up refreshed, with a renewed sense of what's around you.

Play

When was the last time you did something childlike or playful? As we get older, we tend to distance ourselves from play. This attitude is detrimental to creativity, because the ability to see the world through youthful eyes can open doors. Make opportunities to play, especially outdoors. Observe how it feels to be a kid again, as you connect with a part of yourself that's been buried under decades of adult worry.

Good writers are open, not closed. Become more observant—tune into your senses and miss nothing.

Chapter 7

Read Good Writing

*The man who doesn't read good books has no advantage over
the man who can't read them.*

—Mark Twain

If you are going to be a writer, you had better be a reader. Reading
sharpens your thinking, which in turn sharpens your writing. It awakens you
to possibilities and motivates you to write better.

Read everything you can—books, newspapers, magazines, letters, cereal
boxes—both for ideas and to immerse yourself in good writing. Always have
a book going. Peruse different magazines each week. Subscribe to writers'
magazines. Subscribe to at least one newspaper and learn how to skim for
important information. Go online and save electronic copies of relevant
information, or print them and put them in labeled file folders.

As you read, note what works and what doesn't. Sharpen your eye.
Especially analyze the areas in which you struggle—say, dialogue or physical
description.

[See Appendix C, Read Good Writing]

Chapter 8

Keep a Journal

*By writing in a journal every day, you get used to writing
words on paper. You learn to put down on paper what you feel
or think or have observed without inhibition.*
—Irving Wallace

Many people, including plenty of great writers, have kept a regular journal. A journal is a powerful tool for future self-analysis. But it also enriches your life right now.

Keeping a record of your life will hone your writing skills, unleash your creativity, provide insight into your subconscious, and help control stress. Most important of all, it gets you writing. If you have started a journal and quit, it is probably because you made one of the basic mistakes addressed in Appendix C [Keep a Journal]

When choosing a notebook, consider whether you'll be carrying it in your pocket, purse, briefcase, or backpack. Do you want to be able to tear out or rearrange pages? Do you want big pages or small? Lined or unlined?

Review your journal occasionally and look for growth—and there will be growth. Carry it everywhere, so it's handy for those unexpected discoveries, those epiphanies and serendipities. Or carry paper and pen, and then transfer your notes when you return home. Remember, the longer you wait to record something, the more will slip through the cracks of your memory.

Your journal may include:

- Observations

- Experiences

- Feelings

- Descriptions

- Dialogue

- Brainstorming lists

- Reminders

- Story ideas

- Reactions to things you read

- New words, interesting images, wordplay

- Freewriting exercises

[See Appendix D, Keep a Journal]

Chapter 9

Set Manageable Goals

When I face the desolate impossibility of writing 500 pages, a sick sense of failure falls on me, and I know I can never do it. Then gradually, I write one page and then another. One day's works is all I can permit myself to contemplate.

—John Steinbeck

The title of Anne Lamott's memoir of the writing life, *Bird by Bird*, derives from an incident when she was growing up. Her brother, anguishing over a school project on birds, complained, "There are too many birds." Their father, also a writer, advised, "Just take it bird by bird."

To would-be writers who say: "I don't know where to begin," I borrow from Lamott: "Just take it story by story." Don't worry about chronology—you can put the vignettes in order later. Choose an emotional moment from your past and just do the scene. Then do the next one.

Setting out to write a novel-length memoir is much like trying to run a thousand miles. You can't do it at once. But if you run three miles a day, you will reach your goal in a year. So it is with writing. If you aim for a page a day, you will have 365 first-draft pages in a year. Try for 500 words a day; or even 250. As long as you make yourself write every day or so, it won't matter if the word count is low. You will progress. And soon you will become accustomed to setting aside daily writing time.

Chapter 10

Commit to the Truth

To thine own self be true.

—Polonious

The question "What's fair game in a memoir?" comes up a lot. Can you, for example, use dialogue to recreate the verbal brawl that broke up your family decades ago, even though you don't recall the exact words spoken then?

The answer: Yes.

No one can, with tape-recorder precision, bring forth the exact words of any conversation in the recent or distant past. But that doesn't mean you can't include the conversation in your memoir.

If you remember the essence of a scene—say, the screaming insults hurled that time your father came home stinking drunk and Mom made him sleep in the tree house—it is fodder for your scene. Write the dialogue as you best remember it; have the words come out of your characters' mouths.

No reasonable person believes that the dialogue you attribute to your brother sixty years ago is accurate to the word. But if you succeed in capturing the emotional essence of the moment, if you show the characters in action and speech, you will 1) temporarily suspend our disbelief, and 2) allow us to know your brother in some important way.

To be clear, if you're calling your work a memoir, you may not say your childhood house burned down if there was no fire. And you may not, as James Frey did in *A Million Little Pieces*, say you set a county record for blood-alcohol level, got beat up by the Ohio cops, and went to prison for three months if none of those things happened. That's fiction and should be so identified.

On the other hand, you may recreate scenes as you recall them. You're writing memoir, not history.

Chapter 11

Strive to Improve

*Once in seven years I burn all my sermons; for it is a shame
if I cannot write better sermons now than I did seven years
ago.*

—John Wesley

You may be an excellent writer right now, but even so, do you doubt that if
you work hard you will be better in five years? The point is, you always have
growth potential—as long as you stay open to change. Here are some possible
strategies for improving your game:

- Ask people you trust to read your work. Be prepared for criticism.
  Learn from it, even when you don't agree.

- Join a writer's club, which can offer support and constructive
  criticism.

- Take writing classes. Author Irving Wallace credits a Berkeley school,
  The Williams Institute, for his development. Wallace believes the value
  of writing classes is that they "stimulate the newcomer to write, they
  force him to write, and the better ones help him see what is right or
  wrong about what he has written."

- Learn the fundamentals of grammar and punctuation.

- Read a wide range of good writing. Study the work of writers who
  interest you.

- Take journalism courses, which teach you to write under pressure and to meet deadlines.

- Find or hire a personal editor to critique your work. Few are qualified to do the job. You need someone who has both a command of the language and the temperament to tell you when your work needs . . . work.

- Concentrate at first on the free forms of prose, such as letters, diaries, journals, reminiscences, memoirs, or family history. Dismiss the thought of publication at first. You want fluency, not fame.

- Learn to use a keyboard.

Exercise

Pull something out of the drawer that you wrote years ago. Now edit it, noting how your skills have improved. Or have they? If you've been writing, you're certainly better. Have you been writing?

As long as there are postmen, life will have zest.

—William James

Chapter 12

Stifle Your Censor

Censorship in any form is the enemy of creativity,
since it cuts off the life blood of creativity: ideas.

—Allan Jenkins

Writing is hard enough without some scold sitting on your shoulder, finger-wagging a warning: "You better not say that about Uncle Ferg—it makes him look mean (or dishonest or unattractive or . . .)."

If you heed that voice, you will stunt your growth and cripple your creativity. And you will suck much of the fun out of writing.

In your early drafts, which are for your eyes only, why censor at all? Address the sensitive issues only if you publish—that is, take your work public. When you read the piece to a group or show it to others, consider changing names to protect the guilty and innocent.

If you find a larger audience for your writing—say in a magazine or book—and you worry that changing Uncle Ferg's name is not enough to camouflage him, then ask yourself some questions:

- Are you telling the truth as you know it?

- Is what Uncle Ferg did interesting?

- Is it relevant or integral to the themes you want to develop in your memoir?

- Will exposing Uncle Ferg hurt people still living? How much?

- Where does your greater loyalty lie—with your story or with Uncle Ferg?

Don't lose sight of the fact that Uncle Ferg is interesting, at least in part, because of his flaws and foibles. They may not make him lovable, but they do make him human. And if you can redeem him, even slightly, with some good qualities, we will come to care about him.

Bear in mind, a sanitized life is not a compelling life.

Chapter 13

Think Memoir, Not Autobiography

Write about your childhood . . . Write about the time in your life when you were so intensely interested in the world, when your powers of observation were at their most acute, when you felt things so deeply.

—Anne Lamott

"I want to write my autobiography," new students often declare. Invariably they mean they want to write their memoirs.

Autobiography is for Churchill and Roosevelt; memoir is for Hans Deutsch, an inner-city plumber who was mugged or robbed six times, or Barbara Berg, who ran a drill press for twenty years. In other words, ordinary people who have stories to tell.

Memoirs are written memories clustered around a theme. The theme may be life on a farm, travel, career, a city, the theater, any aspect of life. Memoirs tell of particular times or episodes throughout life. They are not narratives of a whole long life history, for that is autobiography. Instead, they are selected parts: the trips, the farm, the jobs, the stage, the war, and of course the people. A memoir can be as long as a page, a chapter, or a book.

Memoir writers use the first person, the "I," to relate and link selected stories of their own past, to tug the reader, to show what it was like as a young fighter jock, an inner-city schoolteacher, a small-town merchant. A retired commodities trader might write about life in the Pit, a stage mother about her talented, troubled child, a grandfather about how he discovered love late in life.

Chapter 14

Master Basic Grammar and Punctuation

*Grammar is a piano I play by ear. All I know
about grammar is its power.*

—Joan Didion

Admittedly, some writers never master the mechanics of English. But they are rare and provide no excuse for the rest of us to ignore the nuts and bolts of our language. If a writer's first goal is clarity, then the means to that end is the mastery of grammar, punctuation, and spelling. Ignore them at your peril, for the result is bound to be muddled writing and sinking credibility.

Some wonder if the rules of writing apply anymore in this age of "how r u?" e-mails. Indeed they do. Readers must be able to understand your scribblings quickly, without excessive labor. They shouldn't have to struggle to untangle the meaning, and most won't have the patience to read on if they start to lose that meaning.

Think punctuation isn't important? Meaning can turn on a comma:

A woman without her man is nothing.

Make two punctuation changes and the meaning makes a seismic shift:

A woman: without her, man is nothing.

Don't be a Slave to Grammar Software

Be cautious about relying too heavily on computer grammar programs. Consider that Lincoln's Gettysburg Address, regarded as one of the most eloquent pieces of prose ever written, gets a flunking grade from RightWriter, a program that checks grammar, syntax, word usage, sentence length, and other elements.

The program considers the first sentence—"Four score and seven years ago . . ."—too long at 29 words, and suggests it be split into two sentences. And, of course, the phrase "all men are created equal" is criticized because it's in the passive voice.

According to RightWriter, Lincoln's writing "can be made more direct by using the active voice, shorter sentences, fewer weak phrases, and more positive wording."

[See Appendix E, Master Basic Grammar]

Chapter 15

Become a Competent Speller

Bad spellers of the world, untie!

—Anonymous

There is no quicker way to lose credibility with your readers than to present a paper rife with spelling errors. Once you start paying attention to correct and incorrect spellings, you will improve quickly. You'll develop a sense of whether a word "looks right." If you work on a computer, you probably have a spell-check program, but don't lean too heavily on that crutch. Spell-check will be silent in the face of a blown homonym. If you write, "His hare turned white . . ." your program will think you're a creative genius.

Some tips:

- Be vigilant and look up troublesome words in the dictionary. Note spelling patterns.

- Learn prefixes and suffixes. For example, once you know that "tele" means "distance," you know television means distance plus vision. If you know that "port" is "carry," you have a head start on the meanings and spellings of teleporter, porter, transport, portable, and other such words.

- Use a mnemonic aid. For example, I learned the meaning of *bellicose*—warlike—by associating it with Nikita Khrushchev's big belly. And I never forgot the meaning of *celerity*—rapidity—once I saw a cartoon stalk of celery at the wheel of a racecar.

- Write out the words you frequently misspell ten times, reading aloud the letters as you write.

[See Appendix F, Learn to Spell]

STARTING YOUR
LIFE STORIES

Chapter 16

Sit Down

The art of writing is the art of applying the seat of the pants
to the seat of the chair.

—Mary Heaton Vorse

The easiest way to start is just to . . . begin. Sit down with paper and pen or pencil. Or sit at a keyboard. That's the way to start—by sitting, prepared, with the tools you need.

You are more prepared than you realize. You already have the tools of the trade, the words you will use. Every kind of autobiography or memoir deals in words, and in English we have nearly a million at our disposal. (According to the Global Language Monitor, English adds a new word every 98 minutes.)

But don't worry—you know more than enough to tell your stories. And words can be changed. Sentences and paragraphs can be deleted. Nothing you write is indelible. False starts and dead ends are common even for experienced writers.

Of course, you need a story; but you have plenty of those, too. Which one should you tell first? Start with an emotional incident rife with conflict, an essential ingredient of drama.

Select a moment, an incident that may have taken an hour or two, not an ongoing crisis. Write about a day when things exploded in your marriage, not about years of marital erosion. If you want people to read your work, you have to tell stories, produce scenes, and make us care about the people inhabiting those scenes. So choose a specific incident that made someone laugh or cry or rage. Then just tell the story, with dialogue and emotion and conflict and humor and a likeable narrator.

Other tips:

- As you begin to write the scenes of your life, disregard chronology. Be led by emotion. Write the stories that interest you first. Give each its own folder and put them in order later.

- Try starting with words such as: "One day in 1968 . . ." or "One sleety November morning . . ." Then keep going. What happened on that day? Tell your story as you'd tell it sitting around a campfire with your friends, using simple language and strong verbs. You might end up with one page or ten. Later, when you edit, you can consider crafting a more gripping lead; but it has served its purpose—forcing you to focus on a specific moment.

- Start with action, not rumination. Pick the most intriguing place in your story to begin, not necessarily the chronological beginning. It may take several drafts before you find that spot.

- Present a situation so vital to the protagonist that we must read on.

- Go where the story takes you.

- Let the story carry your message; don't overanalyze.

- Gracefully accept what Anne Lamott calls "shitty first drafts."

Exercise

Choose a specific emotional incident from your past, distant or recent. Now write that incident as a scene. Stay specific—challenge any generalities. Include dialogue, and don't shy away from conflict. Resist the temptation to editorialize.

Chapter 17

Strive for Clarity

I never understand anything until I've written about it.

–Horace Walpole

The quickest way to lose your readers is through vague or unclear writing. Clarity is the most important quality of tight, interesting writing. No matter how concise your language, how impeccable your spelling and grammar, how gripping your topic—if what you've written isn't clear, you might as well have penned it in Sanskrit.

We're reminded of the importance of clarity when we don't see it, as in this sentence contributed by the Plain English Campaign, an independent group that campaigns against clichés, jargon, and obfuscation: "We are currently experiencing an issue which is impacting the appearance of availability for some seller offerings."

Or in this one: "We are leveraging our messaging leadership to ensure a commercially viable transition path to a high volume, robust and innovative IMS messaging architecture."

If the creators of those masterpieces had shown their work to others, maybe someone would have pointed out that it was unintelligible. But maybe not.

Clear writing starts with clear thinking. William Zinsser cites the president of a major university who wrote a letter to calm the alumni after a bout of campus unrest in the Sixties:

You are probably aware that we have been experiencing very considerable potentially explosive expressions of dissatisfaction on issues only partially related.

He meant that the students had been hassling them about different things.

Here's another contribution from the Plain English Campaign:

Before: "If there are any points on which you require explanation or further particulars we shall be glad to furnish such additional details as may be required by telephone."

After: "Please call if you have any questions."

Clarity can, at least temporarily, elude the best of writers. Because we know what we meant to say, we can become blind to creeping ambiguity. But what we meant to say doesn't matter—only what we wrote.

Exercise

To help determine whether your own writing is clear, 1) read it aloud with a keen ear and a critical mind; 2) show it to others—preferably members of your target audience; and 3) read and edit the piece many, many times.

Chapter 18

Simplify . . . Simplify

*My aim is to put down on paper what I see and what I feel in
the best and simplest way.*

–Ernest Hemingway

When I first sat down to write for publication, my thinking went like this:
"I have no experience, no credits, only an above-average vocabulary; so I
better use a lot of big words to show it off." And I did—for a while. I once
described a merchant in a Bombay [now Mumbai] market as "insouciant."
Today I would probably call her carefree or indifferent—or better yet, show
her, through action and dialogue, revealing those qualities.

Anyway, I was wrong to strive, self-consciously, for a style. Let your style
develop naturally as you learn the craft. The goal, as Nathaniel Hawthorne
said, is "to make the words absolutely disappear into the thought."

Emphasize Short Words

"Simplify, simplify," Henry David Thoreau advised us. Unless you're a
lawyer or a writer for a scholarly journal, you don't have to dazzle anyone
with big words. Beginning writers, especially, must fight the urge to use a
25-cent word when a dime one will do. Legalisms, technical terms and foreign
expressions are constantly entering our language—but that doesn't mean you
should use them with any regularity. Longer words often look self-conscious
and forced. They should be used sparingly, like spice.

Say a character tells another character: "Go to hell!" Or: "I love you."
Three little syllables, but what emotional punch they pack. Perhaps you can
imagine some powerful two-syllable sentences.

Remember, not all synonyms mean exactly the same thing. Don't say *love* when you mean *infatuation*, but if two words do convey the same meaning, choose the shorter one. Say what you mean in the clearest, cleanest, plainest way you can. Strive to eliminate the fat, the fuzzy, the fatuous, and the fancy. For the most part, shun Latinates like *accomplish* and *purchase* and embrace Anglo-Saxon words like *do* and *buy*.

Exception: If one of your characters tends to pontificate in George Will-like fashion, be faithful to his speech, which may be peppered with Latinates. Similarly, a cop testifying in your courtroom scene will likely say *individual* rather than *person*, and *vehicle* instead of *car*. But when your narrator is speaking to us, keep the language simple.

Example

Change	To
accomplish	do
attempt	try
consume	eat
beverage	drink
demonstrate	show
depart	leave
expenditure	cost
inhabit	live
initial	first
remit	pay
require	need
sufficient	enough
transpire	happen
utilize	use
vehicle	car/truck/bus

Exercises

Read Ernest Hemingway's work and note the power generated by one-syllable words.

Write a short action sequence using only one- and two-syllable words.

[See Appendix G, Strive for Simplicity]

Chapter 19

Be Concise

The most valuable of all talents is that of never using two words when one will do.

–Thomas Jefferson

"Clutter is the disease of American writing," says memoir maven William Zinsser. Because good writing is concise, you should strive to eliminate all unnecessary sentences, phrases, words, even syllables. When in doubt, delete and see if the passage reads better. If not, you can always restore it.

Especially scrutinize every adverb. Can you strengthen the verb and eliminate the modifier? For example: "She went quickly to the door" would be stronger and more concise with a better verb: "She darted to the door." Every time the word *very* creeps into your prose, a red flag should unfurl. Look to cut or modify.

Following are common wordy phrases with concise alternatives:

Cluttered	Concise	Cluttered	Concise
great in size	great	in relation to	about
twenty in number	twenty	referred to as	called
personal friend	friend	in view of the fact that	as
with regard to	about	with the exception of	except
all of a sudden	suddenly	thought to himself	thought
at the present time	now	until such a time	until
on the subject of	about	prior to the start of	before

completely filled	filled	seems to be	is
during the time that	while	red in color	red
for the purpose of	for	in order to	to

Omit needless words. Vigorous writing is concise.
A sentence should contain no unnecessary words,
a paragraph no unnecessary sentences, for the same
reason that a drawing should have no unnecessary
lines and a machine no unnecessary parts.

—William Strunk, Jr.

Exercise

Comb your writing for wordy expressions and revise or cut them.

Chapter 20

Craft Gripping Leads

*The last thing we decide in writing a book
is what to put first.*

—Blaise Pascal

Readers tend to remember the beginning and the ending of what they read (the Laws of Primacy and Recency). But the writer who fails to craft a gripping lead won't have to worry about an ending, for the readers will have left long before. As Elmer Wheeler wrote, "Tell it in the first ten words, or you won't get a chance to use the next ten thousand."

The purpose of the lead is to catch the interest of the reader and to indicate, at least generally, what the reader can expect from here on. Your lead should be accurate, brief, simple, informative, clear, and energetic; it should speak to the reader and provide context. Think of your piece as an inverted pyramid: the most important information is presented first, followed by the second most important, and so on.

Whatever lead you choose for a piece, it must:

- Capture the reader's interest.

- Introduce the subject or problem.

- Move smoothly into the body of your piece.

Common lead types

- State a problem.

- Use an interesting quotation.

- Ask the reader a direct question.

- Offer an interesting or unusual fact.

- Offer an alarming or surprising statistic.

- Relate an anecdote or joke.

- Offer an exaggeration of a common situation.

- Show a problem or conflict characters have.

- Show action, in which a character is doing something related to the problem.

- Start with dialogue in which characters are talking about a problem.

- Create a sense of foreboding, a feeling that something important (the problem) is about to happen.

- Depict a humorous situation.

Leads are flashlights that shine down into the story.

—John McPhee

Example

Here is how Frank McCourt began his best-selling memoir, *Angela's Ashes*. What, if anything, about this lead makes you want to read on?

> *When I look back on my childhood I wonder how I managed to survive at all. It was, of course, a miserable childhood: the happy childhood is hardly worth your while. Worse than the ordinary miserable childhood is the miserable Irish childhood, and worse yet is the miserable Irish Catholic childhood.*

[See Appendix H, Craft Gripping Leads]

Chapter 21

Tell Stories

Storytelling reveals meaning without committing
the error of defining it.

—Hannah Arendt

If you want people to read your memoirs, you must become a good storyteller. Organize your life by scenes and give each one its own folder. Don't worry about chronology—you can put them in order later.

Instead of trying to write a narrator-driven autobiography ("I was born here, I went to school there . . ."), focus on specific incidents that happened at a particular time. Rather than write about your marriage, write about a day in your marriage; or your first day on a job. Rather than write about a war, write about a soldier in battle.

Think of yourself as a filmmaker shooting the scenes of your life. What stories do you want to tell? What themes do you want to develop? Now identify which scenes will best help you accomplish that.

Let's say you want to show us how isolated children are in modern society compared to those halcyon days growing up in Chicago, circa 1930. Take us back there, where the streets were crawling with busy kids. Give the characters voices. Let us see the stickball games, hear the sound of the Good Humor man's bell, smell the sweet aroma of grilling bratwurst. If you set the scene and show us you and your friends in full-throated action, you won't have to tell us that children were less isolated way back when. You showed it—and we got the message.

Ideally, your scenes include conflict, emotion, dialogue and, when appropriate, a dash of humor.

[See Appendix I, Be a Storyteller]

Chapter 22

Establish the Setting

*We read five words on the first page of a really good novel
and we begin to forget that we are reading printed words on
a page; we begin to see images.*

—John Gardner

If your words are going to trigger mental snapshots for your readers, you better set the scene clearly, and right from the start. Your parents are arguing—we feel the heat from the dialogue—but where are they? In a car? In their bedroom? Standing or sitting? Those details sharpen the focus of our personal snapshots.

In your early drafts, you might lead with a dateline, such as: "Brooklyn, 1945, The Hollister Apartment." That establishes time and place, lest you lose your way. Later you might work the setting into the prose, or decide to leave it as is.

You don't need to describe your setting in elaborate detail. Offer a few salient features and readers will use their imagination to fill in the blanks. But give them something.

Example

Let's look at two ways to tell the same story. It's a familiar one—a childhood visit to Grandma's. In the first version, the setting is delayed and murky:

> *Every Sunday, my whole family had to visit Grandmother. We children always complained and mother always reminded us the ordeal would last only about fifteen minutes, then we would*

be free. Sitting on the scratchy wool chairs, we waited to endure Grandmother's questioning . . .

Here, the setting is clear from the opening sentence:

I'm seven years old, squirming in my chair. The wool seat scratches against my bare legs. It's bad enough we have to visit Grandmother, but it's even worse, to be here, dressed up and wearing shoes, when we could be in our fort . . .

When I wrote the lead for my profile of rock climber John Bachar, I knew immediately I'd nailed it. Now I realize what I nailed was the setting, the place.

On a soon-to-be-hot September morning in Yosemite Valley, free soloist John Bachar laces on his climbing boots and stares intently at the sheer granite wall that towers before him. He closes his eyes and pictures himself climbing one of its 250-foot vertical routes, the one called "Crack-A-Go-Go." Its polished surface is marred only by a few tiny irregularities and two dime-thin vertical cracks.

Chapter 23

Mix in Dialogue

Don't say the woman screamed;
bring her on and let her scream.

—Mark Twain

Dialogue is one of the truly effective ways to develop a scene and reveal character. Most kinds of writing will accommodate—and be enhanced by—some dialogue. As Anne Lamott writes in *Bird by Bird*: "Dialogue is the way to nail character . . . In the right hands, dialogue can move things along in a way that will leave you breathless."

In other words, what your character says . . . says a lot about your character. Moreover, dialogue offers readers a break from your narrator. Narration tends to tell; dialogue tends to show. [See chapter 29]

Yet, for reasons not always clear, amateur memoirists often shun dialogue. Instead of bringing their characters on stage, they hand the narrator the microphone and let him/her tell us what happened. The narrator explains to the reader what the characters would've said had they been available to speak, a weaker form of storytelling.

Of course, not every word spoken is appropriate for your dialogue. If two characters meet, all the "hi-how-are-yous" should probably be omitted or summarized, as in: "Tom and Jerry greeted each other warmly, like the cellmates they once were."

When determining whether to use dialogue, be guided by the answers to two questions: 1) Would dialogue advance the story? 2) Would it reveal or develop character? If you answer no to both, the material is probably more suitable for narrative summary than for dialogue.

Here are some tips for developing a facility for dialogue:

- Start eavesdropping. Listen in on conversations, not so much for content as for accent, word choice, dialect, pacing, and so on.

- Apply the talk test. When you read over your dialogue, ask yourself: "Would this person actually say that in conversation?"

- Read your dialogue aloud. Hearing your dialogue read aloud is a reality check for stilted language, big words, vagaries, and blather.

- Hide your thesaurus. A thesaurus is a great tool, but it should be used only in emergencies. Use it too often and you'll find words like *pulchritudinous* creeping into your prose.

Pitfalls

Avoid the following:

- Stilted language. Dialogue that doesn't sound like natural speech.

- Filler. Dialogue that doesn't further the scene or deepen our understanding of the characters.

- Exposition. Dialogue in which the character explains the plot or repeats information for the benefit of the audience.

- Naming. Having one character repeatedly use another character's name to establish identity. Except for used-car salesmen, people seldom say other people's names back to them.

- Overuse of modifiers. Minimize the use of dialogue modifiers, such as shouted, exclaimed, cried, whispered, stammered, opined, insinuated, hedged, and countless others. Although modifiers are occasionally useful, too many are annoying, serving only as a crutch for poorly constructed dialogue. Similarly, avoid puny modifiers known as Tom Swifties: "The doctor had to remove my left ventricle," said Tom half-heartedly.

Exercise

Re-read some of your stories, looking for conflict. Now ask: Have I shown conflict through dialogue and action? Or is the narrator just describing it? Look for provocative but insipid passages such as "My parents argued violently that night," and convert them into dialogue-driven scenes. Let us hear the words and feel the heat.

[See Appendix J, Mix in Dialogue]

Chapter 24

Elicit Emotions

How can you write if you can't cry?

–Ring Lardner

Don't shy away from emotional content in your writing. Events that elicit anger, joy, and sadness grip the reader, adding depth and interest to the story. It is emotion that allows your audience to root for or against your characters—that is, to care about them. In the absence of emotion, you risk presenting a dry recitation of facts. You went to the store, you bought some milk, you met a friend, you played golf . . .

Show the reader how you and others felt about events. "I hurled my putter into the creek" is better than "I was mad." Try to show us the physical indicators of strong emotion: breathless, nauseated, slumped shoulders, grinding teeth, tensed jaw, quivering, sweating, shivering, crying, rapid heartbeat, headache, or lack of appetite.

Exercises

Here are some writing prompts bound to elicit emotions. Try to show the character's anger or loneliness through words and actions instead of telling us about it.

- The dumbest thing I ever did

- The loneliest time of my life

- One of life's embarrassing moments

- What scared the life out of me as a child

- The time I ran away from home

- My first date

- If only . . .

- It was the chance of a lifetime

- It rained and rained and rained

- Goofs I'd rather forget

- How I reduce anger and increase love

- Frustrations, frustrations, frustrations

- I didn't think I'd survive

- One time I had too much to drink

- It was a narrow escape

- I've never been so disappointed

- I was so nervous I was shaking

- I had never known anyone who died

- I was so proud

- Was I ever lucky

- A random act of kindness

- What a place for car trouble

- A time I was unjustly punished

- This time I should have been punished

Chapter 25

Pique the Senses

Some books are to be tasted, others to be swallowed, and some few to be chewed and digested.

–Francis Bacon

Let's say you're trying to describe the hot, teeming streets of Bombay. You want the reader to see the sights, yes, but also to smell the sweat and smoke and incense, to taste the curry, to feel the human crush. And so, to make the scene vivid, you must get beyond sight and describe the setting in terms of all five senses: sound, smell, taste, touch, and sight.

If you were describing a circus, you might bring the scene to life by including the smell of popping popcorn; the sounds of trumpeting elephants, roaring cats, and calliope whistles; and the taste of a hot dog.

You add meaning to your sensory description if you let your characters not merely experience all five senses but also react to their experience. In the example below, from Tom Wolfe's bestseller *A Man in Full*, note that the author does not provide the description, but rather the character perceives it. It's the difference between "The air smelled of magnolia" and "Ellen breathed in the scent of magnolia; it always reminded her of her college days in North Carolina . . ." The second is personalized. Because it happens to a character, it is more intimate and immediate, and we care more.

Sensory material will have more meaning for the reader if it means something to one of your characters. The smell of acacia in bloom has greater meaning if someone suffers asthma attacks from acacia.

Finally, you must do all this with light strokes. Most readers will not even notice that you have personalized and unified the story in this way, but they will be drawn into the story by your skills nonetheless.

Example

From *A Man in Full*, by Tom Wolfe

> *As he hobbled on his aluminum crutches toward the Big House,*
> *black gnats were dive-bombing his eyes in waves, without any*
> *letup. Why the eyes? Probably the water. They wanted to drink*
> *the water out of his eyes. Because of his crutches, he couldn't lift*
> *his hands high enough to shoo them away. Now he could hear*
> *them singing in his ears. In the summertime, South Georgia*
> *bowed down helplessly, abjectly, to her rulers, the insects . . . .*
>
> *"That sound," said Serena, "is that the—whuhhhh whuhhhhh*
> *whuhhhhh whuhhhh—sound of them eating?"*
>
> *"Yep," said Charlie.*
>
> *They did make a sort of crunch crunch sound. In fact, it was*
> *the sound of them defecating, the sound of the droppings of tens*
> *of thousands of tent caterpillars hitting the ground.*

Were your senses piqued? Did you hear those bugs? Feel the irritation? In this same scene Wolff goes on to describe the pungent odor of millipedes crushed on the sidewalk.

[See Appendix K, Pique the Senses]

Chapter 26

Write About People

I read and walked for miles at night along the beach,
writing bad blank verse and searching endlessly for someone
wonderful who would step out of the darkness and change my
life. It never crossed my mind that that person could be me.

−Anna Quindlen

All good storytellers offer up characters for us to care about. People, after all, need to identify with other people. If you want to build a story around a snail, give him or her human qualities, as Walt Disney might. Otherwise we simply can't identify with an invertebrate.

Stan once wrote a piece about a woman who kept a caged tiger in her living room. He made the tiger the focus of the story, but I cared much more about that convention-defying woman than I did the tiger, magnificent though it was. If you want us to care about an animal, you better anthropomorphize him, in the manner of, say, Tony the Tiger.

When writing life stories, you won't create characters as a novelist does, but you still must make countless decisions about how to portray your people. Your goal is to make the reader see them as you do.

Ideally you know how they walk, talk, and act; what they love and hate; what they value above all else. You know their motives, understand their frustrations, and identify with their struggles.

Now you must clothe them, give them voices, and sharpen their speech. They must stand out distinctly from each other.

Characterization is hard work. Start by poring through old photos and letters. Interview living relatives and acquaintances, and their acquaintances. Try to remember, and take notes when you do.

Find your quiet spot and reflect on the time the rope swing broke, launching cousin Tex into the river. Or that Thanksgiving when Aunt Linda went after Uncle Tim with a carving knife. Ask questions and look for answers. Compile files on the people you intend to write about.

How to Reveal Character

You can reveal your characters to readers in three basic ways:

1. Through Action

   A. What the character does

   Example 1: Lila steals a pie.

   Example 2: The building is on fire, and Emily rushes in to save her little sister.

   B. What the character says

   Example 3: "I think we can do it," Reid said, looking up at the mountain.

   Example 4: "We'll never make it," Sara said, looking up at the mountain.

   C. What other characters say or think about a character.

   Example 5: "Madeleine is one person you can count on," said Zoe.

2. Through Description

   Example 6: Emily's brown hair curled down to her shoulders.

   Example 7: Mark's muscles bulged as he helped his father move the couch.

   Example 8: Pat's eyes were cold and blue, and he talked like the bad guy in an old Western—slowly between gritted teeth, as though he had a toothache.

3. Through Thoughts

Example 9: I'll never pass that test, Caroline thought, sighing. It's hopeless.

Example 10: Barbara thought of the upcoming swim meet. There's no way I'll let Lee beat me.

[See Appendix L, Reveal Your Characters]

Chapter 27

Embrace Conflict

The greatest conflicts are not between two people but between one person and himself.

–Garth Brooks

The most boring relationships are the ones with no problems. He loved her, she loved him, and they never fought—boring. Readers need conflict.

Conflict is the struggle between opposing forces. A combination of external and internal complications conspire to keep the character from achieving what he/she desires, needs, or must achieve. Whether conflict consists of emotional or physical challenges, it erects barriers between characters and their goals.

All interesting characters have goals—things they want to achieve. As they try to reach those goals, they are blocked by others, the environment, or their own limitations. Trying to overcome those obstacles puts the characters in conflict.

Conflict should make the story outcome seem uncertain. If the ultimate goal seems a sure thing, then maybe you can create uncertainly about how it will be achieved. Ideally, the opponent should be winning for most of the story, seemingly one step ahead of the hero or heroine. The hero's triumph should appear in doubt, or even impossible.

Conflict is an essential element in any story—that is, if you intend to hold your reader's attention. Conflict opens the door to suspense, and suspense is what keeps the reader turning the pages. A story without conflict is a story without action, suspense, urgency. A stress-free, harmonious existence may make for good living, but it does not make for good writing. As characters try to solve problems in your story, they inevitably find themselves in conflict with a) other people, b) society, c) their environment, or d) themselves. Hollywood movie-makers often take the easy way out and feature physical conflict, but psychological conflict can be more compelling.

Well-developed conflict:

- Makes the goal seem out of reach and the outcome uncertain.

- Introduces an obstacle or a series of obstacles.

- Cannot easily be dealt with or explained away.

- Pits major players against one another, both directly and indirectly—physically, intellectually, and/or emotionally.

- Forces the characters to discover something about themselves.

- Forces the characters to discover something about each other.

- Forces the characters to face their greatest fear.

- Taps into the characters' deepest emotions.

[See Appendix M, Embrace Conflict]

Chapter 28

Use Strong Verbs

The adjective is the enemy of the noun.

–Voltaire

As your primary tools of persuasion and power, think verbs, not adjectives or adverbs. The verb is the most important word in most sentences, a concept no English teacher ever shared with me.

Invigorate your writing by using strong verbs, of which there are many:

build	create	deliver	demand
design	direct	encourage	examine
expand	illustrate	improve	inspect
invigorate	jest	mesmerize	mix
oscillate	persuade	prepare	recommend
repair	retrieve	revitalize	share
shape	simplify	snarl	startle
survey	train	trim	unravel

Avoid Nominalizations. Some writers tend to bury their verbs under nouns and prepositions. Instead of "We discussed . . ." they write, "We held a discussion." The livelier "We agree" is swallowed up by "We are in agreement."

The culprits that aid and abet this smothering are often forms of the verbs *to be, give, have, make,* and *take.* Look out for them in your writing.

Change	To
arrive at a conclusion	conclude
take into consideration	consider
make a determination	determine
make a choice	choose
hold a discussion	discuss
have a suspicion	suspect
have a need	need
be in possession	possess

Avoid Excessive Modifiers. Use a weak verb and you'll be tempted to tack on an adverb, as in: "She went quickly to the door." Because *went* is vague and ineffectual, the author tries to empower it with *quickly*. Best to strengthen the verb itself and drop the modifier. Can you think of a verb that would make the adverb superfluous?

> *Substitute 'damn' every time you're inclined to write 'very.'*
> *Your editor will delete it and the writing will be just as it*
> *should be.*

—Mark Twain

Exercise

Come up with a few of your favorite verbs; include them in a phrase, such as: "The sea *rose* up and *snarled* . . ."

1. ————————————————

2. ————————————————

3. ————————————————

4. ————————————————

5. ————————————————

6. ————————————————

Chapter 29

Show, Don't Tell

Don't tell me the moon is shining; show me the glint of light on broken glass.

—Anton Chekhov

Today's readers, jaded by film and television, are used to "seeing" stories. One reason so many reject novels is that the writer has *told* a story rather than *shown* it. The difference between showing and telling is the difference between your characters coming out on stage to act out their roles and a narrator explaining what the characters would have said and done if they could have been here tonight.

How Do Writers Show?

Dialogue is one good way to show. Another is to emphasize verbs. Adjective-noun combinations tend to tell, while verbs tend to show. In the following examples, the first phrase tells, the second begins to show. loud man . . . man roared shiny coin . . . coin glinted old paint . . . paint peeled sad woman . . . woman wept happy dog . . . dog wagged tail

Add Detail

If you say the dog is happy, you leave it to your readers to fill in the blanks, to decide for themselves how a happy dog looks. But the challenge is to guide your readers through the journey of your life. You want to decide, with precision, what they see. The more detail you offer, the more your vision becomes their vision.

> *Steve jammed a sheet of paper into the typewriter. He picked up a pencil, looked at it, and broke it in half. The time for talk was over—he would go see Tom in person.*

Steve is angry, but the reader isn't told he's angry. Instead, the character is given an angry action. Action is a powerful way to show how a character feels.

Note the emergence of *showing* from *telling* in the following:

Tells: *She made breakfast.*
Shows a bit: *She cracked two eggs into a bowl.*
Shows more: *As the eggs, sunny-side up, crackled in the frying pan, she hummed her favorite hymn.*

As we move from the general to the specific, the picture we are painting comes into focus. We could continue to add detail and show even more, making the visual come alive with more action. The key to any improvement is specificity.

If you write: "Polly loved to dive in her swimming pool," you are telling, not showing. Information is being conveyed to us; we do not see Polly. John Updike, however, shows us Polly by painting word-pictures: *"With clumsy jubilance, Polly hurled her body from the rattling board and surfaced grinning through the kelp of her own hair."*

To determine whether you are telling or showing, ask yourself the following questions:

- Are you letting the reader see?

- Is the author/narrator talking at any point?

- Can you silence the narrator by using an action to show what a character feels?

- Is any character telling another character what we already know?

Pitfalls

Beware of three areas where writers are especially likely to tell rather than show:

- When they tell what happened before the story began.

- When they tell what a character looks like.

- When they tell what a characters feels, sees, hears, smells, touches, and tastes.

Chapter 30

Paint Word Pictures

*The greatest thing in style is to have
a command of metaphor.*

–Aristotle

Writers use imagery to help readers "see in their mind" as they read. Imagery is enhanced by specific details (*yellow tulip* instead of *flower*; *shrill blast of the horn* instead of *sound*) that appeal to one or more of the five senses. Examples of imagery include alliteration, simile, metaphor, and onomatopoeia. Although these techniques can enrich your writing, be careful not to overdo them.

The ability to write strong imagery stems largely from your powers of observation. Train yourself to tune into sensual detail. Strive for mindfulness in the here and now.

Chapter 31

Mix in Metaphors

A good metaphor is something even the police
should keep an eye on

–G. C. Lichtenberg

The metaphor is an important technique for creating images. Unlike similes, which make a comparison using *like* or *as*, metaphors establish an identity without such words. By substituting one concept for another, the author makes an implicit comparison: Summer camp is a zoo . . . the cop is a bull.

Developing a feel for metaphor will elevate your memoir to a new level. The artful use of metaphor allows you to unfold picture after picture, not statement after statement.

Examples

Here are some image-provoking metaphors: the long arm of the law; the dawn of civilization; his praying-mantis body curled over the desk; the burnt oil breath of machinery; love was a weed that flourished in the dark; her mind was a tangle of split ends; his life was a nightmare; his hate was a living thing; the temperament of a hungry grizzly; the seismic fault of his life; I wish I had her sail on my boat; a hard fist of fear grew in her stomach; the clouds were swans gliding across the sky.

Pitfalls

A newspaper printed an article about Sudden Infant Death Syndrome. The subject was heartbreaking, but the reporter broke the mood with this metaphor:

We were so proud when we brought our baby home from the hospital, but three weeks later our joy vanished like ice melting on a warm sidewalk.

Even appropriate comparisons can become ludicrous when strung together in an extended metaphor:

Anger drifted and flickered at the edge of Mary's mind like meteors on a dark night. As she thought about what Rob had done, the anger burned brighter and brighter. Slowly it took shape, then shot into her awareness and finally hit hard, jarring the very essence of her life on impact.

On the other hand, an extended metaphor can be effective if done artfully. Consider this passage from James Patrick Kelly's story "Faith":

Faith was about to cross Congress Street with an armload of overdue library books when she was run over by divorce. There was no mistaking Chuck's cranberry BMW 325I idling at the light—except that Chuck was supposed to be in Hartford. The woman next to him had enough blonde hair to stuff a pillow. The light changed and the BMW accelerated through the intersection. Chuck was crazy if he thought he could get away with hit-and-run. The blonde suddenly looked ill; she folded down into her seat like a Barbie doll in a microwave. Without thinking, Faith hurled the top book in her stack. Whump! It was the first time she had ever appreciated Stephen King's wordiness; The Tommy-knockers bounced off the passenger door, denting it nicely. Chuck raced up Islington and out of her life. The book lay open next to the curb. Its pages fluttered in the wind, waving good-bye to fifteen years of marriage.

Exercises

- Evaluate the extended metaphor above. What works? What doesn't?

- Create three original metaphors. Use when appropriate.

Chapter 32

Show with Similes

In argument similes are like songs in love; they describe much, but prove nothing.

—Franz Kafka

Similes are comparisons that show how two things, dissimilar in most ways, are similar in one important way. Similes are a way to describe something. Authors use them to make their writing more interesting or provocative.

Similes, unlike metaphors, use the words *as* or *like* to make a connection between two things being compared.

Examples

- *Playing chess with Zoe is like trying to outsmart a computer.* The activity "playing chess with Zoe" is being compared to "trying to outsmart a computer." The point is that Zoe can think in a powerful manner that resembles the way a computer operates, not that she is like a computer in any other way.

- *His temper was as explosive as a volcano.* His temper is being compared to a volcano in that it can be sudden and violent.

Failed Similes/Metaphors

There's nothing clunkier than a metaphor or simile that misses its mark. Here are some tragic examples from high school essays:

- She grew on him like she was a colony of E coli and he was a room-temperature Canadian beef.

- He was as tall as a six-foot-three-inch tree.

- McBride fell 12 stories, hitting the pavement like a Hefty bag filled with vegetable soup.

- The plan was simple, like my brother-in-law Phil. But unlike Phil, this plan might work.

- The young fighter had a hungry look, the kind you get from not eating for a while.

- She walked into my office like a centipede with 98 missing legs.

- John and Mary had never met. They were like two hummingbirds who had also never met.

- Shots rang out, as shots are wont to do.

Exercise

Underline the word or phrase that is being described by each simile. Put parentheses around the word or phrase it is being compared to. The first three have been done for you.

- Lila frowned and said, "I believe that <u>taking drugs</u> is like (playing with fire)."

- I walked along the beach and listened to the ocean. My <u>sadness</u> was as unending as the (waves).

- Don't tell Mother that her <u>cookies</u> taste like (lumps of sand).

- Mark waited impatiently for his older brother to calm down. "Bill, I think you are acting like a baby," he said.

- Karen was offended when I said that she was as flaky as a snowstorm.

- Be careful when you go out. The sidewalk is as slippery as greased glass.

- I'm not comfortable with this situation. I feel like a bug sitting under a magnifying glass.

Chapter 33

Add Alliteration

*Who often, but without success, have prayed for apt
alliteration's artful aid.*

—Charles Churchill

Alliteration is the use of word combinations that contain the same sounds. It is often used in advertising to catch the reader's attention:

- Finding Facts Fast

- Write right! A Desk Drawer Digest

- Maximum muscle flexibility

Alliteration is also used by serious writers trying to strike a certain mood: slumped into morose musings; the gray-green gloom of the ocean; a miasmic mist; a lazy laughter; bold, black eyes; a camellia-like complexion; a sizzling girl of summer; her hair framing her face; glistening with golden streaks; darkly beautiful but deadly; a short, plump polyp of a man; prominent patrician nose; her common sense skittered into the shadows.

Mix Alliteration with Other Imagery

Sometimes alliteration can be mixed effectively with other types of imagery, as with the following similes: pointing his pipe like a pistol; as quick and quiet as a ferret; as bleak as a battlefield; rough sea winds that swept like lost souls.

Pitfalls

Alliteration is like sugar—too much can give us a toothache. Witness these examples from a children's book:

- The mild-mannered monkeys did not seem at all frightened of the ferocious feline.

- The big, brown bear was very entertaining as she proudly performed bouncy, ballet steps while balancing on a ball.

Exercises

- Look through books and magazines and find two examples of alliteration. Are they effective? Why?

- Create five alliterative phrases that wouldn't embarrass you in your next story.

Chapter 34

Dabble in Onomatopoeia

. . . With a moo moo here and a moo moo there
Here a moo, there a moo, everywhere a moo moo . . .

—from the song, "Old MacDonald Had a Farm"

Onomatopoeic words suggest the sounds they describe. They appeal to our sense of hearing. Bees buzz, cows moo, and lions roar. As with all imagery, however, you must be careful not to overuse them. Too many cows mooing and lions roaring can create white noise for the reader.

Some common onomatopoetic words:

Swish, hiss, sizzle

Honk, neigh, hoot

Splash, clang, twang

Moo, coo, meow

Bang, thud, thump

Slurp, fizz, tinkle

Growl, grunt, howl

Exercise

How many onomatopoetic words can you add?

1. _____

2. _____

3. _____

4. _____

Chapter 35

Favor the Active Voice

*A writer is a person for whom writing is more difficult
than it is for other people.*

–Thomas Mann

Assertive writing is direct and crisp, unburdened by lifeless verbs, excessive qualifiers, and the passive voice. The voice is active if the subject of the sentence is the "doer." For example: "I bought the book." The active voice is almost always more direct, more economical, and more forceful than the passive.

Passive voice adds words and subtracts clarity. In the passive voice, the subject is acted upon: "The book was bought (by me)." Look for the verb "was" in your writing; it often signals the passive voice.

Sometimes the passive voice is justified—for example, "The Golden Gate Bridge was built during the 1930s." We may not care who built the bridge, only *when* it was built. But when you use the passive voice sentence after sentence, it's like killing your characters.

One of my students wrote a piece about growing up on a farm in Illinois. Describing the nuts and bolts of farm work, she strung together six straight passive sentences: "The cows were milked . . . The hay was baled . . ." But no one was on stage actually milking or baling; it was just being done. Readers need finely etched characters doing the action, characters they can see and care about.

Examples

Passive: A new safety record was established by me for my department.

Active: I established a new safety record for my department.

Passive: The multiplication tables were learned by Nadia in the fifth grade.

Active: Nadia learned the multiplication tables in the fifth grade.

Passive: In addition, the annual fund-raising dance was coordinated by me.

Active: In addition, I coordinated the fund-raising dance.

[See Appendix O, Favor the Active Voice]

Chapter 36

Shun Clichés

Never use a metaphor, simile, or other figure of speech which you are used to seeing in print.

—George Orwell

The first time someone wrote, "Claudius is as fat as a pig," readers probably ooohed and aahed over the rapierlike precision of that simile; today it's a tired cliché.

Clichés are expressions that have been used so much in writing and speaking that they are familiar to readers—too familiar. Clichés make communication stale and boring. Root them out whenever you find them in your writing.

Rewrite "quick as a flash," "as plain as day," and "last but not least" as "quickly," "clearly," and "finally." Even better, make the effort and create an original simile or metaphor that eliminates the adverb and turns the sentence into a real gem.

Example

Unless you are portraying a character prone to uttering banalities, avoid the following expressions—and countless others like them: add insult to injury; green with envy; in the same boat; weigh a ton; on cloud nine; busy as a bee; grinning from ear to ear; white as a ghost; calm before the storm; in a jiffy; at death's door; not a second too soon; in this day and age; heart on her sleeve; one in a million.

Exercise

Choose three clichés, put them in a paragraph, then rewrite them as original expressions.

Chapter 37

Root Out Redundancy

When I see a paragraph shrinking under my eyes, like a strip of bacon in a skillet, I know I'm on the right track.

–Peter de Vries

I used to read a book to my daughter, entitled *Alexander and the Terrible, Horrible No Good Very Bad Day* (Judith Viorst). That, my friends, is redundancy.

Redundancy comes from a Latin word meaning "to overflow." In English it means excessive, unnecessary, wordy, repetitive. When writing term papers for school, you called it padding. Whatever you call it, get rid of it. That's what editing is for.

An editor—whether you or someone else—strives to cut unnecessary words without losing meaning. It's a skill that can be honed with practice, and by paying close attention to what good editors do with your prose.

Can you spot any redundancy in this sentence? *I was in charge throughout the entire project.*

The word *throughout* makes *entire* unnecessary. You could write: *I was in charge throughout the project.* But inserting a better verb also improves it: *I remained in charge of the project.*

Exercise

Correct the following sentences to eliminate the redundancy:

1. Submission of applications must be timely and punctual.

   _____

2. This is only my personal opinion.

   _____

3. We cannot approve of the changes in any way, shape, or form.

   _____

4. Unless and until we hear from you.

   _____

5. The instructions were not clearly legible.

   _____

Chapter 38

Omit Nonessential Detail

I didn't have time to write a short letter,
so I wrote a long one instead.

—Mark Twain

Herb recently wrote his own obituary. In the first paragraph, he told us the name of the train he took to California prior to starting a new job. But he never identified the job. Although deciding which information to include in your memoir can be a highly personal one, can anyone reasonably argue that the name of the train is more important than our hero's new career?

Another student, Sasha, wrote a piece in which she included her childhood address and phone number. Such mundane information only detracted from her story; she would have been better served cutting it, footnoting it, or relocating it in an appendix. Readers can then look it up if they're interested.

When Herb was asked by his classmates why he included the tedious logistics of traveling from one city to another, he replied, "Because it happened." But a writer must make decisions. The material you choose to include should advance the story, or at least be interesting in its own right.

If clarity is your first goal, then holding your audience's interest is your second. It doesn't matter what you write if no one wants to read it. So know your readers and try to anticipate and target their interests.

Consider following the example of Elmore Leonard, who says he tries to leave out the parts that readers tend to skip.

Chapter 39

Overcome Your Biases

Lawyers, I suppose, were children once.

—Charles Lamb

Two of my former students were sailors at Pearl Harbor on December 7, 1941—and both turned their memories of it into a mind-numbing recitation of facts.

They were analytical types, more at home describing the nuts and bolts of their ships than the human drama unfolding before them. The result: their stories were bloodless, bereft of smoke, fire, explosions, screaming, suffering, death, and thus life.

To write memoir (or fiction), you must care about people. You must put the spotlight on humans and make machinery and other inanimate objects the backdrop. Keep in mind William Zinsser's four basic premises of writing: clarity, brevity, simplicity, and humanity.

Professional Limitations. All other things equal, caregivers, social workers, and teachers have an easier time humanizing their life stories than accountants, engineers, and attorneys. In my experience, lawyers, especially, struggle to overcome the inherent limitations of their profession. After years of billing by the syllable, many have a tendency to be wordy, redundant, pedantic. Now retired and wanting to pass on their "autobiography," they believe their main task is to convey information rather than to tell a gripping story. They aim to write their life stories as they once wrote legal briefs—packed with persuasive facts.

But memoirists are not trying to win an argument or sway a jury; they are trying to win over their readers by writing life stories that people want to read.

Gender Limitations. Many splendid male writers have put pen to paper, so this is another generalization: *Men have more trouble handling emotional content than women do.*

Taught from an early age to be strong, silent types—that is, to show little emotion—many men bring a stoicism to their stories that sucks the life right out of their writing.

Just because you didn't cry when your father whipped you doesn't mean you felt nothing. Go inside and find what's there. As a storyteller, it's your task, your challenge, to tap into that emotional content and move the reader. Make us feel your sadness, anger, resolve.

Chapter 40

Do the Research

If you steal from one author it's plagiarism;
if you steal from many it's research.

—Wilson Mizner

Even if you're writing your own life stories, you won't know everything. How old was I when I contracted polio? Mom might know. What was the score of the championship game? Maybe Coach knows.

Get used to querying people who might have the answers you need. Email makes that easier than ever. Most people will be flattered that you asked, especially if they know the answer. Such exchanges will not only refresh your recollection but spawn new ideas.

Your quest for accuracy should sometimes send you to the library or to a search engine. Take Jean, who wrote that her uncle had once completed a marathon. "Imagine," she went on, "Uncle Mort, who had never completed anything in his life, went 25 miles without alcohol once touching his lips . . ."

That's pretty good stuff, except that a marathon is 26 miles and change. It's certainly no disgrace that Jean didn't know the exact distance. And she was right not to interrupt the creative flow over such a technical point. But eventually she needs to recognize her uncertainty and get it right.

About two seconds on Google ought to do it.

Chapter 41

Find the Humor

*People are never so trivial as when
they take themselves seriously.*

—Oscar Wilde

Humor isn't right for every writer. Some of us simply lack the requisite wit. Moreover, certain subjects—the Holocaust comes to mind—would seem to lack a lighter side.

Yet Shakespeare was able to interject comic relief into the most tragic of his plays. And most great fiction writers, no matter how grim their subject, remember to give their readers occasional cause to smile or laugh.

Here are three simple ways to elicit laughs:

- Surprise.

- Exaggeration/Embellishment.

- Comedic timing.

Surprise. As your story progresses, readers will make predictions about where you are taking them. A sudden change in direction shocks us and may provoke a laugh.

Exaggeration/Embellishment. Exaggeration is a familiar way of drawing laughs. In the movie *Annie Hall*, when Woody Allen announced to Annie that she had a spider in the bathroom "as big as a Buick," he was exaggerating for humor.

Bill Bryson used the same technique in his memoir, *The Life and Times of the Thunderbolt Kid*, when he described his dentist as about 108 years old with more than a touch of Parkinsonism in his wobbly hands. [see Appendix O]

Comedic timing. Before comedians utter a punch line, they usually pause. The equivalent for the humor writer is to create a new paragraph, even if only two or three words long.

By moving the punch line to its own paragraph, you give the reader a chance to take a breath. At the end of the punch-line paragraph, the reader has another break to laugh (you hope) before continuing the story. For example:

> *John was so obese, he had to shop in stores with names like Mr. Humongous. Normal menswear stores carry sizes like Large, Extra Large, and sometimes Extra Extra Large. Mr. Humongous had sizes like Two-Man Tent and Canopy. Shopping at Mr. Humongous allowed John to feel good about himself. There, he was one of the smaller sizes. On his last visit, he'd seen someone buy an 8XL leather coat.*
>
> *Making it put an entire species into extinction.*

Family life can be a great source of humorous material, as Erma Bombeck repeatedly showed in her prolific career.

> *When you are feeding teenage boys, you know you are in deep trouble when you run out of food before you've finished taking the groceries out of the car.*

Don't force the humor, and don't overdo it. Humor is much more subjective than drama, but that's no reason not to try, especially in early drafts. Take some chances and go for the laugh—you can always cut it later.

[See Appendix P, Find the Humor]

Keeping Momentum

Chapter 42

Revise . . . Revise . . . Revise

I'm not a very good writer,
but I'm an excellent rewriter.

—James Michener

Ernest Hemingway believed "the value of a book can be judged by the value of what is thrown away." And Hemingway threw a lot away. He once confessed that he had rewritten the last page of *Farewell to Arms* thirty-nine times before he was satisfied. "What was it that had you stumped?" asked a journalist. "Getting the words right," he replied.

And when novelist Bernard Malamud said, "I would write a book, or a short story, at least three times: once to understand it, the second time to improve the prose, and a third to compel it to say what it still must say," he was talking only about rewriting, not about the far more numerous editing trips he made through his manuscripts.

Writing is too difficult to expect to get it right the first time. Fortunately, we deal in ink, not oils. Deleting is not only allowed, it's essential. I show no one my work before its time—fifth draft at least. Although many people can write better first drafts than I do, few can craft a first draft superior to my fifth draft.

You must edit . . . then edit some more. If you have the time, put the manuscript away for a week or so, then go through it, now with a more objective, ruthless eye. Take out everything that doesn't belong. Buff what's left until it shines. Repeat as necessary.

As Anne Lamott says, don't be afraid to write crappy first drafts—no one is going to read them. Perhaps we should say, no one *should* read them. All too often, new writers read, show, or submit first or second drafts. I blame school, where we first learn to go public with imperfect work.

Yet only after a few drafts does our work begin to glitter. In revision lies excellence. Go find it.

Here's the blueprint, according to novelist Sidney Sheldon:

- Take an idea you really, really like.

- Develop it until it is brilliant.

- Rewrite it for a year or two, until every word shines.

- Then bite your nails, hold your breath, and pray like mad.

As your experience grows you will find that revising is pleasurable, even though its purpose is the discovery of your own failings.

—Jacques Barzun

[See Appendix Q, Revise Your Work]

Chapter 43

Craft Titles to Stay on Track

*I want to write books that unlock
the traffic jam in everybody's head.*

—John Updike

Marilyn Dennis and her husband have been flying together in small planes for fifty years. Marilyn recently read a piece in class about a rough flight from Santa Rosa, California, to Oregon. She entitled it "Mt. Shasta," which is the dominant landmark en route.

Although Marilyn is a good writer and the piece has enormous potential (a close call in a small plane?), the story lacked a precise focus. I suggested the problem began with the title. "Why not call it 'The Scariest Flight,' or something like that? Then, when you get off track—and we all get off track—just glance at the top of the page to regain your focus."

My memoir students are forever tacking on poetic titles such as "The Golden Statue" or "A New England Autumn." Euphonious though they may be, such titles don't help the writer maintain deep focus. Besides, you don't really want to write about a New England autumn; you want to write about that November in Maine when you fell out of love.

Make your titles specific. For example, "The time I almost drowned in Lake Fondue, November 1947." Clunky, you say. So what? Your writing group doesn't care what you call your piece, so make the title work for you. Even if it rises to a magazine piece, editors will decide what to call it.

Make it clear from the start what you're writing about. Consider titles that put you and the reader in a specific moment—and keep you on track: "The day my brother gave me a black eye" . . ."I thought I'd die on that hike" . . ."How Uncle Ernie lost his leg on Okinawa."

Exercise

Go through your memoir chapters, decide what each story is really about, and title or retitle as needed. Now evaluate the focus and organization of each story with the new title in mind. Did you tell the story you wanted to?

Chapter 44

Choose Good Topics

Memory is a child walking along a seashore. You never can tell what small pebble it will pick up and store away among its treasured things.

—Pierce Harris

When choosing memoir topics, your life is your canvas. If an event or experience had an impact on you—especially an emotional one—it's fodder for your stories.

Many storytellers fall into the trap of describing general conditions. Because you went to camp every summer for five years, you start throwing *woulds* around: "We *would* go down to the lake every morning" . . ."I would ride my bike to town." Better to cover a specific trip to the lake, the time you learned to swim . . . or almost drowned . . . or were nearly eaten by crocodiles.

In other words, craft scenes that put the spotlight on specific people, including yourself, caught up in emotional events.

For example, you might write about a time you, or someone you know:
Shivered in fright
Felt lonely
Swelled with pride
Did a dumb thing
Took a risk
Ran away
Went on your first date
Started a romance
Fell in love

Had the chance of a lifetime
Goofed
Blushed in embarrassment
Were surprised
Felt nervous
Made an important decision
Erupted in anger
Cried
Laughed
Felt frustrated
Thought death was near
Wanted to kill someone
Got drunk
Lost a friend
Had a narrow escape
Behaved badly
Felt disappointed
Got revenge
Had no money
Grieved over a death
Achieved a goal
Reached a turning point
Made a smart decision
Loved a child
Got lucky
Kicked a bad habit
Felt regret

[See Appendix R, Choose Good Topics]

Chapter 45

Develop New Ideas

*I never understand anything
until I have written about it.*

–Horace Walpole

Ideas are in ready supply. The challenge is to latch onto them and make them work for you. Here are some ways to widen the pipeline of new ideas:

Keep a journal. Review your entries for new ideas. Play around with form, style, character, and viewpoint. These experiments will often shake loose new ideas.

Follow your emotions. What gets you worked up—fiction? nonfiction? airplanes? scuba diving? List the things you really care about. What thrills, infuriates, astounds, terrifies, excites, shocks, disturbs, or embarrasses you? The more strongly or deeply you respond to a subject, the more it means to you, the more you will have to say about it, and the more intensely you will say it.

Be observant. Tune into the obvious, and the not-so-obvious. Change your routine; do things that force you to see the world from new perspectives, as though for the first time, as a child might. Or try to see the world through the eyes of another writer—say, a poet or an historian. Watch a loving or quarreling couple and imagine their conversation from both points of view. Role play, pretending you're the pilot, the soda jerk, the victim, the victor.
Dr. David Reuben conceived his wildly successful sex manual, *Everything You Always Wanted to Know about Sex but Were Afraid to Ask*, while observing honeymooners in Acapulco. Said Reuben: "I'd see them arrive with this

just-married glow. And then, the next morning, they might not even be talking to each other. I realized they were completely unprepared."

Brainstorm with others. Grapple over ideas with writers, yes, but also with other intelligent, creative people you trust. Afterward, write in your journal and note the new ideas that crop up.

Read good writing. Peruse newspapers, magazines, books, and the Internet for ideas. Subscribe to writers' magazines. Learn how to skim for important material. Visit libraries, and photocopy relevant material. Start files of clippings from your sources.

Talk to authorities. If you want to include something in your story about the Greenhouse Effect, you better chat it up with scientists. If you plan to set a scene at the Indianapolis Speedway, you better engage with a few drivers and greasy pit-crew guys. When I wanted extra information on the intestinal parasite *giardia*, I contacted the Centers for Disease Control in Atlanta as well as local public-health agencies. As you interview your authorities, be alert to new ideas.

Freewrite. Write uninhibitedly for 5, 10, or 15 minutes at a time. If you get stuck, write the same word over and over until you unstick. Or insert an ellipsis and write, "What I really want to say is . . ." and go on writing. Keep your hand moving and let your imagination go. Deliberately fantasize. Follow your hunches and intuition. Stretch your mind. Lose control and forget about grammar and punctuation. Find your wild mind, and watch the ideas flow.

Mine conversations for material. One writer, after a fight with his wife, raced to his typewriter and wrote out the angry dialogue. And many others have eavesdropped on the conversations of strangers and used the material in their work.

Talk with people, particularly people outside of your usual circle. Get them to tell you about their jobs, their childhoods, their families, their values. You may have to prod with specific questions, but in general do more listening than talking. Pay attention not only to what people say, but how they say it.

Mine other sources for material. My first book, *RISK! An Exploration into the Lives of Athletes on the Edge*, was inspired by a movie entitled *Heart Like A Wheel*, the story of drag-racing champion, Shirley "Cha-Cha" Muldowny. The movie provoked two questions: 1) Why does someone go into an off-beat sport like drag racing? and 2) What skills are necessary to excel? Driven by this curiosity, I went on to profile dozens of high-achieving athletes for four books.

Ask questions. What has always fascinated you? Outer space? The sex life of moles? What would you like to read that hasn't been written? Confirm by looking through *Books in Print*.

Browse through unusual sources. Check out your mother's high school yearbook . . . the Paris Yellow Pages . . . the obituaries . . .

Live it up. Experience new places. Travel. Visit a shoelace factory . . . a fishing boat . . . a bocce tournament . . .

Chapter 46

Eliminate Unworkable Ideas

*Genius is one percent inspiration and
ninety-nine percent perspiration.*

—Thomas Edison

I once put in dozens of hours working on a manuscript about flea markets. Blinded by some amusing stories I'd heard about those events, I thought I could turn them into a book. Then one day it hit me: I don't like flea markets.

What I had was not a book, but an idea—and a bad one at that. Bad for me, that is, because my passions lay elsewhere. And that's the point: Follow your passions; do what you love; put the rest aside.

If you catch the writing fever, you will no doubt produce more ideas than you can handle. The challenge then is to eliminate those with the least potential. First, ask some important questions:

- What type of material is it? Is there enough human interest in it?

- Is there a theme to hold it together?

- How important is the idea? Will it influence the groups I'm interested in reaching?

- How original is the idea? Have I read it in other places? Is it just now being talked about?

- How costly and time consuming is the research likely to be?

- Will the material interest me and others for a long time?

Exercise

What subject has made you think, "Somebody should write a book about that"? Describe that can't-miss idea in a couple of paragraphs. Consider pursuing it further.

Chapter 47

Learn to Take Criticism

The covers of this book are too far apart.

–Ambrose Bierce

If you're going to get beyond journal writing—that is, take your work public—you're going to have to solicit, and then try to benefit from, criticism. Most of us struggle with the latter and become defensive. But awareness and practice will make you more receptive to constructive criticism.

In my writing classes, we have what we call the Rosemary Rule, named after my student Rosemary Manchester, who has the rare ability to both absorb and deflect criticism. Typically she nods and says pleasantly, "Thanks, I'll think about that."

It's the ideal response, because as author you are final arbiter. Your personal editors can only make suggestions, which you need not heed. Having said that, don't miss the opportunity to learn from the opinions of others. Take criticism as a warning that something is wrong, at least in the eyes of that one critic. When you say, "I'll think about it," really think about it.

But how do you know if what others say has merit? Mystery writer Elizabeth George advises us to "go within," adding:

> You can spend your entire life writing and rewriting the same first chapter if you listen to other people's opinions and ignore the one sure place where you will always find the truth: in your own body.
>
> When you are telling the story you are meant to tell, you are actually going to feel the truth of it, and in feeling that truth,

your spirits are going to soar. When you are telling that story the way it needs to be told—through the kind of writing you can be proud of—you are going to feel that as well. If you become aware of that feeling of sureness, soundness, and wholeness that develops inside you when you are on the right track, then you won't be led astray by anyone else's opinion.

That doesn't mean you should listen to no one. It means you choose your critics carefully, and when what they say has the ring of truth to it, try it out and see if it *feels* like truth.

[See Appendix S, The Art of Critique]

Chapter 48

Break Through Writer's Block

Writing is no trouble: you just jot down ideas as they occur to you. The jotting is simplicity itself—it's the occurring which is difficult.

—Stephen Leacock

Writer's block, when the brain freezes and the fingers cramp into ineffectual claws can drive us to despair. Disturbing questions hound the blocked writer: "Is it over?" "Have I passed my creative peak?" "Will I ever write again?"

Writer's block can strike anybody at any time. What to do?

- Don't panic. You may be afflicted by writer's block in the first place because you are worried, distracted, or depressed. Don't make it worse by dwelling on your inability to write. Failure then becomes a self-fulfilling prophesy.

- Check for external pressures, such as physical or emotional stress, illness, poor diet, inadequate sleep, excessive distractions, or changes or disruptions in your routine. Fix or eliminate as much as possible.

- Change where, when, or how you write. Use pen and paper instead of computer, or write in the early morning instead of at night. Use more or less light; keep a coffee pot going; write in bed or the bathtub.

- Have several different projects going at the same time. When you block on one, put it away and pick up another one. It may be easier to work on a fourth draft of project B than a first draft of project A.

- Work on something other than the lead. Agonizing over a story's lead may be the number-one cause of writer's block. The lead is often the hardest part to write. Even under ideal conditions, you may not be able to write the lead until you've told the rest of the story. But if you're blocked, you should definitely return to it later.

- Stay alert to fresh ideas when you're not blocked. Compile notes and start file folders on possible future projects. Then, when blocked, you have something new to work on.

- Write outside of your usual genre. Writing fiction or poetry can rejuvenate.

- Do a timed freewrite. Even a five- or ten-minute freewrite can unclog the pipes.

- Regain the flow by writing letters. Many writers warm up every day by writing letters.

- Focus quietly for a minute or two on the spot where you're stuck. Let your mind wander wherever it wants to roam; such wanderings often lead to something useful.

- Write in your journal. You may even create something—a character sketch, a dialogue—that you can use in one of your stories. If not, at least you've written.

- Keep writing, even if you're seemingly going nowhere. Let the piece wander or lose its way for awhile. If necessary, write nonsense—but keep going. Continue to push ahead until something clicks.

- Look through old photographs. Pictures elicit memories, which can be turned into scenes. You might start by composing captions.

- Brainstorm with other people. Invite and consider fresh perspectives and ideas.

- Meditate and then return to your piece.

- Retype your last page, and then keep right on going.

- Rewrite the troublesome section—this time with a different point of view, time, setting, dilemma, or narrator.

- Reward yourself once you finish a project, or a part of a project.

- Go play. See a movie, visit a friend, take a walk. While your conscious mind is off duty, your subconscious mind will continue to plug away. Although it's unwise to give in regularly to the voice urging you away from your desk, sometimes a prolonged break can refuel your creative juices. After consulting your doctor, mix exercise into your play. Even a brisk walk will sharpen attentiveness, reduce stress, and build stamina. You'll write longer and with greater focus.

- Get enough sleep. Study after study has confirmed what you already know: insufficient sleep dulls your senses and stunts your creativity.

[See Appendix T, Freewrite Through Writer's Block]

Chapter 49

Mine Available Resources

I don't have to look up my family tree,
because I know that I'm the sap.

—Fred Allen

Consider resources and techniques that can add variety and human interest to your stories:

- Letters. Extract quotes or reproduce letters entirely. Merge them into one of your episodes or include them in an appendix.

- Diary. If you've kept a journal or have access to one written by a family member, pull pertinent quotes from it. Tell us when and where the words were penned. Weave them creatively into your text.

- Family sayings. Quote those quaint phrases you heard as a kid. If your father's mantra was "anything worth doing is worth doing well," then have him utter those words. Show us the family's reaction to them.

- Poetry. Add verse at the beginning, middle, or end of an episode. It's a nice creative touch if it's your own poetry, but it's not essential. Give credit if you use someone else's words. For publication, you must obtain the author's permission unless the work is in the public domain.

- Clippings. Look for old newspaper clippings, such as wedding announcements, news stories, and obituaries. Insert them in appropriate chapters or in an appendix.

- Photos. Include important photos in your memoirs. Digital photography makes this ever easier.

- Documents. Birth and marriage certificates, wedding announcements, diplomas, commendations, or other special papers may be included in appropriate chapters or in an appendix.

- Musical lyrics. If you danced to "Puttin' on the Ritz" or swooned to "Blue Moon," you may want to include a stanza or two.

- Family tree. If you have worked up an ancestral chart, you can include it at the beginning or in an appendix.

- Time line. Your life depicted on a continuum can highlight the key events and make it easier for the reader to follow your story. Put it at the beginning or end.

- Maps. Maps can help put the story in geographical context.

- Drawings. If you have the talent, illustrate your own memoirs. If not, perhaps an artistic friend could illustrate a section, chapter, or the cover.

- Statistics. Too many statistics can make your reader's eyes pop out. Offered judiciously, however, they add substance to your writing. The population of your town in 1945, the cost of bread and milk during the Depression, life expectancy when you were born, the dates of events—such facts help the reader gain perspective.

- Recipes. Favorite or important recipes can enrich a piece. When student Ruth Colvin wrote about her mother making soap from scratch, she included the recipe.

- Famous quotes. Include proverbs or quotes by famous people that support a point you want to make. Some writers like to begin each chapter with a provocative quote.

- Opinions. Although you don't want to pontificate, you shouldn't shy from offering opinions on matters important to you, including (but not restricted to) politics, religion, philosophy, law, morality, child rearing, or the Chicago Cubs. Keep a light touch as you weave in messages you want to pass on to future generations.

Chapter 50

Peruse Old Photos

One picture is worth ten thousand words.

—1927 ad

When Joyce Wood needs a memoir topic, she often opens a scrapbook and peruses old photos.

> *Looking at a yellowing, mouse-chewed photo I'd taken of Lake Tanganyika (in Burundi) brought back memories of the genocide soon to come. Then I remembered how the crocs used to eat people bathing in the lake at night. Dozens of story lines came to me just from gazing at that one photo.*

When she found an old photo of herself standing in front of the Kremlin, in Moscow, she went to work. A week later she had crafted a life story about surviving winter days cold enough to freeze urine in midstream.

Photos of friends and family members offer obvious profile possibilities, but remember to show us Uncle Ferg's duplicity or Aunt Ellen's generosity through their actions and speech, instead of pushing your narrator on stage to tell us about those qualities.

Even photos taken by others, of people and places you've never seen, can spark story ideas. A shot of a street urchin panhandling on the streets of Chicago might remind you of a personal experience in Chicago . . . or with a street person . . . or . . .

Chapter 51

Find a Personal Editor

Some editors are failed writers,
but so are most writers.

—T. S. Eliot

Although you must be your own best editor, you also need to show your work to others. More to the point, you must find someone willing and able to read your work with an objective, critical eye. Most people, even your most literate friends, can't help you. Either they will be reluctant to offend or will lack the skills to do so.

Find someone with a critical eye for the language, someone unafraid to speak out, preferably someone who will work for free. Now hang on and don't let go.

That's what I did with Bruce Maxwell, a close friend, a writer himself, with a master's degree in journalism and a sharp editorial eye. When I was profiling adventure athletes, I'd regularly drive two hours to Bruce's home, and together we'd pore over my latest manuscripts, syllable by syllable. It was one of the greatest learning experiences of my life.

That's the point—I learned. Eventually, after about thirty profiles, I gained the skills and confidence to go it alone. Like everyone, I still need editors, but now they wield a scalpel, not a butcher knife. Bruce elevated my game, and I haven't stopped thanking him.

Chapter 52

Link your Stories to History

If you want to understand today,
you have to search yesterday.

—Pearl Buck

You have lived through a time of unprecedented change, so give readers some context by setting your story in its time—the Depression, World War II, the turbulent Sixties. Where were you when Prohibition ended? World War II began? Kennedy was shot? Armstrong walked on the moon?

A student recently wrote, "I turned eighteen the day after the war started, December 7, 1942."

What's wrong with that sentence? We'll let pass that no war is specified, since she clearly means World War II. But World War II began on September 1, 1939, when the Nazis marched into Poland. The writer must be referring to the bombing of Pearl Harbor, but that occurred on December 7, 1941.

Providing historical backdrop to your stories will enrich them, but getting the facts wrong will shred your credibility. After all, if we can't trust you with facts in the public record, how can we trust you to tell personal truths?

Do the research necessary to refresh your recollection and to assure accuracy.

Chapter 53

Become a Capable Interviewer

When people talk, listen completely.
Most people never listen.

–Ernest Hemingway

The interview is at the heart of the writer's research, whether you're writing memoir or fiction. Talking to people also gets you out of yourself, increases respect for human differences, and develops your conversational skills.

When I set out to profile adventure-athletes for my first book, *Risk!*, I was unsure of my interviewing skills. I called a professional writer who had done dozens of interviews and asked his advice. "Don't worry about it," he said. "There's nothing to it—just be conversational."

That was good advice. Relax, be friendly and courteous, ask questions. Most people, unless they've been hounded by the press, will take your attention as a compliment and be happy to talk with you. If you are interviewing a friend or family member, all the better.

Many of your answers will indeed come from Mom or Uncle Richard, and those will likely be easy, informal interviews. But let's say you want to include details about the parasitic worm you got while kayaking the Amazon. You may want to talk to an authority at the Centers for Disease Control; you may have to talk to a stranger.

First and foremost, a good interviewer is a good listener. Pay attention to the answers you get and be prepared to deviate from your script to ask follow-up questions. Although you will get some of your best information from so-called digressions, you may have to gently redirect respondents who roam too far from your line of questioning.

No matter how good a listener you are, you will have to record your subjects' answers on tape or paper. Truman Capote claimed he retained 94 percent of what he heard or read. Few of us approach that figure. Distrustful of my note-taking skills, I rely on a small tape recorder, which frees me to listen and jot down possible follow-up questions. That leaves the tedious task of transcribing tapes, but at least I know I have the respondent's exact words if I need them.

As a courtesy, ask your subjects if they have any objections to your recording the interview—few will. Finally, make sure your recorder is working and that you have backup batteries. Periodically check the machine to see that it's still running.

[See Appendix U, The Art of the Interview]

Chapter 54

Develop Serious Themes

The act of writing inspires me.

–E.M. Forster

Have you ever finished reading a story, announced that you liked it—then never thought about it again? It was fun while it lasted, but provoked no critical thinking—for the simple reason that it raised no issues sufficiently serious or profound to warrant further thought.

Here are examples from four students in my Sebastopol class unafraid to tackle serious themes:

- Ed Feldman recently read a piece in class about his three-month stint doctoring in Nepal, one of the most primitive spots on earth. Although his is a fascinating story in its own right, he added punch by addressing themes, by raising questions about big issues—in this case, cultural differences and the real meaning of altruism.

- Rosemary Manchester is writing about her years in Africa as a missionary wife and mother. In addition to unfolding the compelling drama of raising four children while her husband strove to raise the natives closer to heaven, Rosemary gives weight to her work by tackling cultural, racial, and religious issues.

- When Chuck Kensler was six, he endured a long road trip to Washington with his father, a Lakota Sioux, and his Scottish mother. In his story, Chuck gives us an inside view of the ongoing clash between Native Americans and Europeans, twentieth-century style.

- Gay Bishop is writing about her days working in the animal hospital at the Boston Zoo. Each chapter is devoted to another adorable animal—Satan the Toucan, Sally the Chimp—which is enough to carry the story. But Gay also addresses the larger issue of the role zoos play in our society and whether we and the animals are better for it.

Think of learning to write your life stories as a two-step process of becoming: 1) become a good storyteller, employing the tips in this book, and 2) become adept at grappling with the big issues that provoke your readers to challenge their assumptions about race, religion, class, and our changing times.

PUBLISHING YOUR LIFE STORIES

Introduction

*The two most beautiful words in the English language
are "check enclosed."*

—Dorothy Parker

A commercially publishable memoir needs at least four elements: large-audience appeal; a sympathetic character or two; a thought-provoking, inspirational story; and good writing. Celina Spiegel, co-editorial director at Riverhead Books, says, "No matter how appealing your story, if you're going to write it down, you have to be able to write."

That's why we covered writing skills in the earlier sections. By now you write well, or at least you know what you have to do to write well. Now we'll look at how to get your life stories and other writings into print.

Here is my Blueprint for Publishing Success. The pages that follow provide more details and tips.

The Blueprint

- Love to write; really love to edit. We don't call the first version a rough draft for nothing. If you craft the perfect metaphor or hit the sweet spot with some dialogue, it's probably during editing. When writing for publication, I will do at least six drafts. Some authors make more than twenty-five editorial passes.

- Develop a schedule and commit to write regularly. Write several times a week. Standard advice is to write every day, and that's fine if it works for you. But it may be an unrealistic goal. To give yourself every chance to succeed, aim to write three to five times a week. If you find yourself going weeks without writing, it's time to question your commitment to the craft.

- Write nonfiction. About 90 percent of everything published is nonfiction. After you get a few things in print, you can write the Great American Novel.

- Aspire to write well. Join writing groups, devour how-to-write volumes, subscribe to *Writer's Digest*, read voraciously, seek criticism.

- Find a personal editor. Although you need to be your own best editor, you also need to show your work to others. Beware, though, as most people will do little other than crush or inflate your ego—not what you need right now. Mothers are notoriously, sometimes pathologically, supportive, as are many friends. Find someone with a critical eye for the language, someone not afraid to speak out.

- Prepare to compete. Remember, you're doing battle with television, the greatest time-stealer in history, as well as movies, newspapers, video games, the Internet, and countless other distractions. The good news: A market still exists for good stories well told.

- Be interested in the subject you propose. Any insincerity will be revealed in your writing. What's more, you won't have any fun.

- Come up with marketable ideas. Go to *Books in Print* and find out what has been published on the subject you're considering. Visit your local magazine racks and prowl through periodicals that might be candidates for your work. Call publishers or go online and order back copies of the magazines that interest you.

- Know your audience. Each article should be directed to a specific audience—veterans, feminists, hockey fans. If you want to write for a magazine, peruse ads to gain insights into who reads it. As you write, picture your readers and tailor the article accordingly.

- Be willing to work on speculation at first. Working on "spec" means you do the work with no assurance of ever getting paid. That's how I wrote my first book, *RISK!* The advantage: you have tangible proof of the quality of your work. The disadvantage: your labor may go financially unrewarded.

- Start with local markets. When you send a proposal to an editor, it's sometimes wise to include *tear sheets*—examples of your previously published work. A good way to acquire tear sheets is to contact editors of small, local newspapers, who are always looking for material.

Chapter 55

Crack the Magazine Market

*My point to young writers is to socialize. Don't go up
to a pine cabin all alone and brood. You reach that
stage soon enough anyway.*

—Truman Capote

As you're compiling your life stories, you may find that one or more of them are
appropriate for the magazine market. The magazine market is volatile—periodicals
come and go—but there may be more now than ever. *Sam's Sailing Magazine*
might fold next year, but in the meantime its editors need copy.

Magazines have long been dropping fiction or reducing the number of
short stories they publish. Gone are the days (the Twenties) when F. Scott
Fitzgerald could command $4,000 per story from the *Saturday Evening Post*.
Today, nonfiction rules the magazine world, and some of that content is memoir,
ranging from filler-length anecdotes in, say, *Reader's Digest* to 25,000-word
personal reminiscence pieces in *The New Yorker*.

Tips for Cracking the Magazine Market

- Wear two hats. If you want to sell to magazines, you have to be part
  businessperson, part writer. This can be a challenge, for they demand
  different skill sets, even contrasting ones. Writing is a solitary pursuit;
  marketing your work demands a facility with people.

- Acquire the latest copy of *Writer's Market*. This annual tome lists
  thousands of magazines, including information essential to a
  freelancer: what and when they pay, what they are looking for, when

they respond, contact information, and other submission tips. Highlight any periodical that might be a candidate for one of your pieces; make a list; prioritize.

- Understand the publications you query. Go to their websites and order back copies. In this way you learn which subjects have recently been covered and what type of articles the editors favor. Study the slant, length, opening, and general presentation.

- Adapt to the idiosyncrasies of the magazine. Some magazine writers claim they spend as much time canvassing the market as they do writing.

- Picture your readers. Each article should be slanted toward a specific reader. Perusing a magazine's ads can tell you a lot about your audience, including interests and educational level. Before doing an article, ask yourself 1) Who is my reader? 2) What is my material? 3) What is my purpose in bringing reader and material together? (to amuse, enlighten, prod?) 4) How can I produce the desired effect or response?

- Write a compelling query letter to a specific editor [see Chapter 56]. Your query is both a sales promotion and evidence of your writing skills. Make it sing.

- Follow up. Most editors are swamped with submissions, so don't be surprised or hurt if someone doesn't get back to you on time. Note when your queries go out, when the publication claims it will respond, and be prepared to follow up with phone call or letter at a prescribed time, probably 4-6 weeks later.

- Be prolific. Some magazine writers have dozens of manuscripts making the rounds. Prolific writers don't wait for inspiration.

- Persevere. Professionals keep trying, and this applies to both the writing side and the business side. It's not uncommon for writers to submit a piece to a dozen publications before acceptance. A never-give-up attitude can pay real dividends. Resubmit a piece a few months later and you may find a different editor at the post. Perhaps the magazine's needs have changed. A new staff may buy what a previous staff rejected.

- Include photos. If photography is an interest of yours, this would be a good time to improve your skills, and possibly increase your income. Visualize "Photojournalist" on your business card.

Chapter 56

Write a Compelling Query Letter

Dear Contributor: Thank you for not sending us anything lately. It suits our present needs.

—Note from publisher received by Snoopy in comic strip "Peanuts"

A query letter, or query, is an offer to write an article or book and an attempt to interest an editor or agent in buying or representing it. It is, in other words, a sales pitch.

Instead of writing an entire article that might not be bought, you write a letter about the proposed article or book. Your goal: a commitment to buy, or at least a strong expression of interest. By drumming up sufficient interest in advance, you save yourself the grief of researching and writing things no one wants to publish. Also, by determining which publication is going to publish the finished article, you can more clearly envision and target your readers when you finally write it.

Here is what you should include in your query letter:

- Your idea. What the idea is about. For example: "The Tasadays are the most primitive tribe living in the world today."

- Your slant. "The Tasadays have a more satisfying life than more civilized groups of people."

- Your treatment. Some indication of how you intend to approach the subject. "I will build the article around interviews with several notable Tasadays."

- Sources. Some of the ways you will acquire information. "Several Tasadays have moved into my neighborhood, and I've become friendly with them. Moreover, I have been granted access to the Tasaday cave drawings in the Philippines . . ."

- Make the editor care. "I believe the readers of *Caveman Digest* will be interested in this piece because of their close philosophical ties with the Tasadays. In a recent study of value systems among Cavemen and Tasadays, professor Seth Loo found remarkable similarities between . . ."

- Your writing credits. "My work has appeared in *Firehouse* magazine and *Humpty Dumpty* . . ." Don't write something like "I've never published anything, but . . ." or "I'm taking a writing class and this is my first query." Such remarks will only encourage an editor to reject you.

- Suggested length and deadline. "I propose an article of approximately 2,000 words, and I can deliver it within two months." If the editor likes your idea, she will suggest a length and deadline of her own.

- Other relevant information about yourself. "I am half Tasaday myself, and for three years I was editor-in-chief of a Manila newspaper, where I came in contact with many Tasadays." Avoid this: "I am married, have three children, and a frog named Butch."

Other Tips

- The letter should be brief—no more than two pages; one is better.

- Single-space the letter; double-space between paragraphs.

- Your letter should contain the above information but in no special order. Also, you are not necessarily dead if you leave out one item.

- Most important, make the query interesting. It should entertain, inform, and compel. Most important, it should make the editor want to read on. Make it lively to demonstrate your enthusiasm, factual to demonstrate your knowledge, and well written to demonstrate your talent.

- Use anecdotes, quotes, examples, statistics, questions, jokes, excerpts from other articles, and whatever else it takes to show the editor what you want to write, how you want to write it, why you are the person to write it, and why the editor should care.

- Make the lead grabby, but don't overpromise. Don't write, "The Midwest's greatest tragedy occurred in Sidepork, Iowa, in 1998, and yet few people outside of Sidepork know about it," if the tragedy was a man falling into a vat of chocolate.

- Address the proposal to a specific editor. If your copy of *Writer's Market* is old, or even if it isn't, check a recent masthead or call the publishing house. Spell the editor's name correctly; in fact, spell everything correctly.

- If you have previously published works, include samples. These are called tear sheets. Ideally, they are similar to the writing you are proposing.

- If photos are available, say so.

- Include a self-addressed stamped envelope (SASE).

- Finish politely and affirmatively. "Thank you for your attention. I look forward to hearing from you."

- Make the whole package neat and professional.

Results

- Nothing happens. Wait 4-6 weeks, then write to or call the editor, politely asking for an update.

- Rejection. Most queries are rejected. It's not necessarily a reflection on your work, but simple math. Publishing houses get many more submissions than they can use. You may see two types of rejections: form and letter. In a letter rejection, you may find encouragement in the editor's words, or even advice on how to improve the piece. Listen to it if you can.

- A go-ahead on speculation. This is encouraging—the editor is showing interest—but you have a decision to make. You may write the piece and find the editor still doesn't want it.

- Firm assignment. Write back your acceptance. Open champagne.

Exercise

- Create a query letter to sell an editor on your latest project. Do several drafts; get feedback from others. Polish, polish, polish.

[See Appendix V, Master the Query Letter]

Chapter 57

Collaborate with an Agent

No author dislikes to be edited as much
as he dislikes not to be published.

—Russell Lynes

If you want to persuade someone to publish the words you slave over, you may need a literary agent—or not. I acquired a New York agent early in the game, but he has sold only one of my thirty books. On the other hand, he has been my friend, therapist, guide, and even editor on occasion. So my advice is this: Try to get an agent, but don't depend too much on him or her.

Agents are certainly essential when marketing book-length manuscripts to big-time publishers, such as Random House or Simon & Schuster. But, unless you're John Irving or Stephen King, agents will *not* sell your magazine articles, poetry, or short stories. And if you're trying to sell a book idea to one of the many small, independent presses, you can probably represent yourself as well as an agent can.

That said, literary agents are book-marketing experts who can sell your crafted words to jaded publishing professionals. The right agent can turn a manuscript gathering dust in your drawer into a published book. A reputable agent will work hard to make sure your writing pays what it should. Most important, an agent will improve your chances of escaping the slush piles that threaten to overwhelm the office space of all successful publishers.

Your job is simply to produce writing that an agent can believe in.

[See Appendix W, Collaborate with an Agent]

Chapter 58

Learn from Rejection

To working writers, rejection is like stings to a beekeeper: a painful but necessary part of their vocation. They understand that the return of their work isn't meant as a personal rebuff (or seldom is, anyway). It just feels that way.

—Ralph Keyes

Rejection is to the publishing life as criticism is to the writing life. Both can hurt your feelings, but both offer great opportunities. They are your springboard to improvement.

The key is to keep an open mind and not take rejection personally. Once you do that, a rejection letter becomes a learning tool. When an agent, publisher, or editor turns down your work, probe for their reasons; reevaluate your work with their comments in mind.

It might help to recall some of the accomplished authors who received multiple rejection letters before they published: J.K. Rowling, John Irving, Pearl Buck, Dr. Seuss, Ursula Le Guin, Saul Bellow, Alice Munro, and many others.

Notable Rejections

"Who would want to see a play about an unhappy traveling salesman?" –Cheryl Crawford, Broadway producer, turning down Arthur Miller's play *Death of a Salesman* (and rejecting Elia Kazan's offer to produce it).

"I'm sorry, Mr. Kipling, but you don't know how to use the English language." –Editor at *San Francisco Chronicle*, rejecting a short story by Rudyard Kipling.

"Louis, forget it. No Civil War picture ever made a nickel." –Irving Thalberg, MGM producer—offered film rights to Margaret Mitchell's novel *Gone With The Wind*—to his boss, Louis B. Mayer.

"A long, dull novel about an artist." –1934 letter rejecting Irving Stone's fictional biography of painter Vincent van Gogh, *Lust for Life*. The book went on to sell 25 million copies.

"Regret the American public is not interested in anything on China." –Rejection note to Pearl Buck regarding her manuscript for *The Good Earth*.

"It does not seem to us that you have been wholly successful in working out an admittedly promising idea." –Rejection letter to William Golding for *Lord of the Flies*.

"It will not sell, and it will do immeasurable harm to a growing reputation . . . I recommend that it be buried under a stone for a thousand years." –Rejection letter to Vladimir Nabokov for his novel *Lolita*.

"The girl (Anne Frank) doesn't, it seems to me, have a special perception or feeling which would lift that book above the curiosity level." –Rejection letter for *The Diary of Anne Frank*, the best-selling memoir of all time.

Chapter 59

Avoid Vanity Presses

Vanity is the quicksand of reason.

—George Sand

Vanity presses make their profit charging authors to publish their works, not by selling books. If the author is willing to cough up the money, vanity press will generally agree to print and bind anything not obscene or libelous.

The phrase "cough up" is apt. Nearly all vanity press books sell depressingly few copies and lose money for their authors. According to *Writer's Digest*, vanity-published books rarely return one-quarter of the author's investment. Those few that succeed usually do so because of extensive self-promotion by the author.

Because vanity presses are not selective, publication by a vanity press is typically not seen as conferring the same recognition or prestige as commercial publication. Publishing a book with a vanity press may label you a gullible amateur. It can have a negative impact on your writing career.

By definition, the publisher is whoever pays for the production and distribution of the book. If the author puts up the money, the author is the publisher. Thus, vanity presses are really printers, not publishers.

Chapter 60

Print on Demand

*Writing is the only profession where no one considers you
ridiculous if you earn no money.*

−Jules Renard

Many successful writers have started out by publishing their own
works. In self-publishing, the author puts up the money, takes the risks, but
has near absolute control over the project. Thanks to the development of
computer software, true self-publishing has become easier and less expensive.
Moreover, no stigma attaches to self-publishing, as it does with so-called
vanity presses.

Print on Demand (POD)

When I co-published my first book *RISK!*, in 1986, digital printing didn't
exist. For an initial print run of two thousand books, I had to invest $8,000.
Now, with Print on Demand technology, you can publish your book for a few
hundred dollars and then order books as you need them.

Print on Demand, sometimes called Publish on Demand, is a printing
technology and business process in which new copies of a book are printed
when an order is received. POD developed only after the advent of digital
printing, because it wasn't economical to print single copies using traditional
printing technology, such as letterpress and offset printing.

POD publishers generally do not screen submissions prior to publication.
They accept uploaded digital content as Microsoft Word documents, text
files, or RTF files. Authors choose from a selection of packages, or customize
a printing package that meets their needs. For an additional cost, a POD

publisher may offer services such as cover design, copyediting, proofreading, and marketing. Some offer ISBN (International Standard Book Numbers) service, which allows a title to be searchable and listed for sale on websites.

Many critics dismiss POD as another type of vanity press. One major difference, however, is that POD publishers have a connection to retail outlets like Amazon.com and BooksInPrint.com that vanity presses generally do not.

Before you commit to a POD publisher, do some comparison shopping. Check out their websites, including Xlibris.com, iUniverse.com, and VirtualBookWorm.com.

If you opt to purchase the service of a self-publishing company, as I did with this book, keep in mind that the most basic packages do not include editing and proofreading. They may provide only technical services—printing, binding, and little else. It takes much patience to proofread the many drafts. Everything from correct spelling to accurate pagination is your responsibility. You may have to pay careful attention to layout; a lot of formatting may be lost when the text is converted by the publisher.

Is Self-Publishing Right for You?

The first step is to decide if you and self-publishing are a good fit. Think of self-publishing, including POD, as four distinct but related phases:

- Writing and editing: crafting the manuscript.

- Producing: creating the cover, photos and drawings, text, layout, printing, and binding.

- Promoting: building a need for your book.

- Distributing: getting your book in the right hands.

If you can honestly answer yes to the following questions, you are good to go.

- Are you willing to risk time and money? When I co-published *Risk!*, I had to invest $8,000. I vowed I would not lose money on the project, and I didn't. But it took a lot of work—business work, not writing work.

- Do you want to be a businessperson as well as a writer? Writing is quiet, solitary work; publishing/promoting tends to be active, social work.

- Do you have or can you develop good organizational skills? Those skills must be applied to both the business side and the writing side.

- Do you have the time? Create a grid of the 168 hours in a week. Fill in the nondiscretionary time—sleeping, eating, chores, work. Does enough time remain for you to run a small business? To set regular weekly working hours?

- Do you like to do research? As a self-publisher, you have to research not only writing ideas but also markets for your work.

- Do you have marketing/sales skills? To succeed, self-publishers must be assertive. Are you willing to pitch your book to your friends and family? To wholesalers and distributors? It may require book signings, TV and radio appearances, and other public-relations and marketing strategies.

- Do you have or can you create an office environment? Self-publishing is ideal for a home office, but make sure it's a private place conducive to doing good work.

- Do you like networking? Writers tend to be reclusive types, but as your own publisher, you must talk to people. This may mean attending writers' conferences and workshops.

- Can you prepare a business plan and set a budget? If not, can you learn?

To run a self-publishing business requires little more than the ability to use telephone, fax, and email. To be successful, however, requires much more. You must be willing to invest time and money. You must be open to developing skills and gaining knowledge. And you had better like running a business.

[See Appendix X, Consider Self-Publishing]

Chapter 61

Look to the Next Project

Better to write for yourself and have no public,
than to write for the public and have no self.

–Cyril Connolly

Let's say you finish a piece and send it off to an editor or agent. Now what?

Open the appropriate celebratory bottle—and then get on with your writing life. Approach the mailbox each day with modest expectations. By the time the "no-thanks" begin rolling in, if they do, you will be immersed in new projects, and that will take the sting out of any rejection. If you get an acceptance, open another bottle.

Remember, it's the work that's important. Success, fame, money—they're not the main reason we write . . . right?

Chapter 62

Persevere

I work and I think and I push and I scribble until something comes. When I actually get something to work on, I sit at my typewriter and type until I ache so badly I can't get up.

—Danielle Steel

If you want to improve as a writer, you have to learn to take criticism; if you want to get published, you have to learn to take rejection. Both are inevitable. Your success will largely be determined by how you respond to such adversity. Once you get knocked down, do you get right back up?

The ability to persevere is critical for any amateur writer aiming to turn pro—but also for anyone in pursuit of excellence. Truman Capote took five years to complete *In Cold Blood*. Jonathon Harr worked eight years on *A Civil Action*. Pearl Buck's classic *The Good Earth* was rejected by dozens of publishers.

Here are some other testimonials to the importance of patience and perseverance:

Louis L'Amour, author of more than 100 western novels, with 200 million copies in print, had 200 stories rejected before he made his first sale.

Gone With the Wind, by Margaret Mitchell, was turned down by at least 25 publishers.

Mary Higgins Clark was rejected 40 times before she sold her first story. Today, more than 30 million copies of her books are in print.

Dr. Seuss's first children's book, *And to Think That I Saw It on Mulberry Street*, was rejected by 27 publishers. The 28th publisher, Vanguard Press, sold six million copies.

Chicken Soup for the Soul was rejected by 20 publishers before Health Communications agreed to publish it. Since then 8 million copies of the original book have been sold. The series has grown to 32 titles, in 31 languages, and sold more than 53 million copies.

The manuscript for *Harry Potter and the Philosopher's Stone* was turned down 9 times before hitting pay dirt. J. K. Rowling's *Harry Potter* books went on to sell 325 million over the next 10 years.

What makes perseverance possible?

- Love what you do.

- Believe in what you do.

- Keep doing it.

APPENDICES

Appendix A

Love to Write

In the following memoir/personal essay, entitled "The Invisible Writers," Tai Moses introduces us to soldiers and bakers, convicts, and salesmen, all of whom share the same affliction: They must write. Whether out of love or compulsion is debatable, but the result is, they produce.

The Invisible Writers

Many years ago I knew a grizzled old playwright named Ray. He lived off state disability checks, carried his manuscripts in brown paper bags, and drank cup after cup of black coffee, which I poured for him from behind the counter of the coffee shop where I worked.

He had one piece of advice for me: "Read Othello. If you want to be a writer you must first read Othello."

Ray was a blue-collar guy who had never gone to college, but he had read Shakespeare, checked out from the public library near the furnished room where he lived. Ray understood plot because he had lived and experienced it. He was a born writer.

Over the years I've met a diverse collection of writers who have never been published or earned any academic credentials, yet whose claim to the title of artist is genuine. These invisible writers are soldiers and bakers, convicts and salesmen, winos, hairdressers, firefighters, farmers and waitresses. Their only qualifications to literary authenticity are their writings and their desire to write. Often the only time they have is stolen time, and their private scrawls end up on cocktail napkins, penciled in the margins of receipts, on any piece of paper handy.

I got to know Tom Carson during the first Gulf War, shortly after his platoon had been sent to Kuwait. We never met in person. He had written to a co-worker of mine who had moved on, leaving no forwarding address. When I saw the U.S. military return address on Tom's letter, I decided to answer it myself. We began a correspondence that lasted through the war and after he returned to Fort Benning, Georgia.

During a hectic two months, Lt. Carson wrote 39 poems. His themes were the regimented insanity of military life, isolation and loneliness, the wind and rain of his soul. Carson wrote his lines in rare solitude, in a barracks or a tent. During the day, he told me, the thoughts gathered in his head; he censored them but the forbidden words found expression anyway, for even the U.S. Army cannot discipline the imagination.

People imprisoned in stultifying, menial jobs can summon, with even a minimal command of language, something entirely private, unfettered and incalculably powerful. Most importantly, it is something of their own creation that cannot be taken away. The sense of purpose and identity that comes with being a writer, creator of a private world, can be life altering.

I've known truck drivers who are natural-born storytellers; fishermen who paint starkly beautiful word pictures of life on a crab boat in the Bering Strait. I met a barely literate ex-convict whose short story about losing his wife and child in a revenge killing for a gang crime he'd committed was the most heartbreaking thing I've ever read. I met a recovering alcoholic who wrote about being abandoned by her husband. In a few simple paragraphs this uneducated woman in her mid-50s expressed a universal sense of loss in an entirely unsentimental fashion; something that cannot be taught in any MFA program.

My own father, a novelist who was never published, once wrote about being fired for writing on the job—a chronic problem in his lifetime. He worked on an assembly line in a factory that manufactured radios, and the foreman caught him writing one day while the neglected radio parts moved past him on the belt. "I was only half a radioman," wrote my father. "In my heart, I was a poet."

As Chester Himes wrote in "The Quality of Hurt": "No matter what I did or how I lived, I had considered myself a writer . . . It was my salvation. The world can deny me all other employment, and stone me as an ex-convict . . . as a disagreeable, unpleasant person. But as long as I write whether it's published or not, I'm a writer."

I met Celia at a roadside diner, where she cooked greasy breakfasts for travelers whose faces she'd never again see. Writing, for Celia, was a way of being elsewhere, of undoing, undreaming, her mundane daily life. The monotony of her job and the deadening rituals she performed daily were the inspirations for the poems she scribbled on used order tickets. To hate your job and do nothing about it is a failure of imagination: a true life sentence.

A Frenchman I know who was a maitre d' at one of the Washington's finest restaurants, possesses a novel he composed in the twilight time between the lunch rush and the dinner hour. His joy on writing it was immeasurable. That it may never be published did not faze him. The point is that he created it. He finished it. It is his.

"Fiction completes us, mutilated beings burdened with the awful dichotomy of having only one life and the ability to desire a thousand," Mario Vargas Llosa wrote.

I've often looked for my old playwright friend Ray's name in print, but have never seen it. I imagine him sitting in a coffee shop somewhere, brow furrowed as he revises lines of his latest play, completely absorbed in the world of his characters. I'm sure it frustrated Ray at times, that his work went unrecognized, but it never occurred to him to quit; just like it would never occur to him to stop breathing.

It is not strictly a tragedy that Ray's plays, the maitre d's novel or Celia's poems remain unpublished. Much of the work comes into being for private reasons of the heart. If every sentence that was written was printed and bound we would drown in a sea of words—as it is, thousands of books are hastily published, barely read and forgotten. Writing itself is the aim, for it is writing, not publishing, that transforms individual human experience.

To write, even in obscurity is worthwhile. As Samuel Becket put it, writing is a way of leaving "a stain upon the silence."

Tai Moses is a writer in Oakland, California.

Appendix B

Make Time to Write

Consider two basic ways you can schedule your writing time:

- The Rigid Method

- The Spare-Time Method

The Rigid Method

This involves a rigid schedule that you follow diligently. Lay out a grid that covers every block of time in your week.

1) Fill in every hour that is committed. Include everything you routinely must do and like to do, such as work, taking the grandchildren to school, and sleep.

2) Study the empty blocks on the grid. Fill in the blocks where you are certain you can write. Try for a minimum of three two-hour blocks per week. Five blocks would be better, but be realistic. Give yourself a chance to succeed.

3) If you are unable to find enough hours in the week to write, reevaluate your priorities. Assign each obligation a priority number: 1. Must do; 2. Like to do.

4) Search that second category for any activities that might be sacrificed for the good of your budding writing career.

Once you have a workable schedule, stick to it. Announce to everyone within earshot that this is your writing time and that you don't want to be disturbed except in an emergency. Beginning writers sometimes feel so guilty about their writing time that they cave into demands from their family. Resist! Show others that you take your writing time seriously—and they will take it seriously, too.

The Spare-Time Method

This is a more flexible schedule that allows you to set goals for the week and to choose which times and days you will write. With the Spare-Time Method, your goal is not putting in a specific amount of time, but rather producing a specific number of words or pages each day. All that matters is that you reach that word count. It's still important that you write as often as possible, but when you do the work is up to you.

Each method has its advantages. Choose the one that works best for you.

The Habits of Successful Writers

Drawn from Jill Krementz's book, *The Writer's Desk*, here are ten authors describing their work habits:

E.B. White. "A girl pushing a carpet sweeper under my typewriter table has never annoyed me particularly, nor has it taken my mind off my work, unless the girl was unusually pretty or unusually clumsy. My wife, thank God, has never been protective of me, as, I am told, the wives of some writers are. In consequence, the members of my household never pay the slightest attention to my being a writing man—they make all the noise and fuss they want to. If I get sick of it, I have places I can go."

Bernard Malamud. "You write by sitting down and writing. There's no particular time or place—you suit yourself, your nature. How one works, assuming he's disciplined, doesn't matter. If he or she is not disciplined, no sympathetic magic will help. The trick is to make time—not steal it . . . If the stories come, you get them written, you're on the right track. Eventually everyone learns his or her own best way. The real mystery to crack is you."

Katherine Ann Porter. "I can live a solitary life for months at a time, and it does me good, because I'm working. I just get up bright and early—sometimes at five o'clock—have my black coffee and go to work. In the days when I was taken up with everything else, I used to do a day's work, or housework or whatever I was doing, and then work at night. I worked when I could. But I prefer to get up very early in the morning and work. I don't want to see anybody or speak to anybody. Perfect silence. I work until the vein is out."

Joan Didion. "I need an hour alone before dinner, with a drink, to go over what I've done that day. I can't do it late in the afternoon because I'm too close to it. Also the drink helps. It removes me from the pages. So I spend this hour taking things out and putting other things in. Then I start the next day by redoing all of what I did the day before . . . When I'm really working, I don't like to go out or have anyone to dinner, because then I lose the hour . . . Another thing I need to do, when I'm near the end of the book, is sleep in the same room with it. Somehow the book doesn't leave you when you're asleep right next to it."

Walker Percy. "I think you have to be sitting there. You have to 'wait' in good faith. You have to go to work like anyone else, or I do anyway. I have to go to work at nine o'clock. And in that sense you force it. You've got to start in some way . . . You have to have a routine and live up to it and then hope for the best."

Cathleen Schine. "I love my bed. It is larger than a desk and better designed to hold books and papers. It is softer than a desk and better designed for naps. It is the center of all good things. And, day or night, everyone knows where to find me."

James A. Michener. "When I am about to start a major project, I am much like a Zen master in Japan who is about to serve a ritual tea. I wash my face, cleanse my mind, eat sparingly, exercise every evening by taking long walks, go to bed early and rise at seven to go to my typewriter. I do this seven days a week for the two years during which I am doing the actual writing, and I am loathe to permit interruptions. In the morning I do not welcome either visitors or phone calls because writing is hard, exhausting work, and at twelve-thirty when I stop, I am usually sweaty."

Tennessee Williams. "In Key West I get up just before daybreak, as a rule. I like being completely alone in the house in the kitchen when I have my coffee and ruminate on what I'm going to work on. I usually have two or three pieces of work going at the same time, and then I decide which to work on that day . . . I go to my studio. I usually have some wine there. And then I carefully go over what I wrote the day before. You see, baby, after a glass or two of wine I'm inclined to extravagance. I'm inclined to excesses because I drink while I'm writing, so I'll blue pencil a lot the next day. Then I sit down, and I begin to write."

Ann Petry. "It doesn't much matter where I sit to write. The first draft is in my head. The next draft is in longhand on paper, and after that, I type it. All along the way I make changes. The final draft bears very little resemblance to whatever it was I had in my head."

Joseph Heller. "I have to be alone. A bus is good. Or walking the dog. Brushing my teeth is marvelous—it was especially so for *Catch 22*. Often when I am very tired, just before going to bed, while washing my face and brushing my teeth, my mind gets very clear and produces a line for the next day's work, or some idea way ahead. I don't get my best ideas while actually writing."

Appendix C

Read Good Writing

Need a reading list? To get you started, here's the Modern Library's list of the 100 best nonfiction and fiction books written in English and published in the 20ᵗʰ Century:

Nonfiction

1. *The Education of Henry Adams,* Henry Adams

2. *The Varieties of Religious Experience,* William James

3. *Up from Slavery,* Booker T. Washington

4. *A Room of One's Own,* Virginia Woolf

5. *Silent Spring,* Rachel Carson

6. *Selected Essays, 1917-1932,* T. S. Eliot

7. *The Double Helix,* James D. Watson

8. *Speak, Memory,* Vladimir Nabokov

9. *The American Language,* H. L. Mencken

10. *The General Theory of Employment, Interest, and Money*, John Maynard Keynes

11. *The Lives of a Cell*, Thomas Lewis

12. *The Frontier in American History*, Frederick Jackson Turner

13. *Black Boy*, Richard Wright

14. *Aspects of the Novel*, E. M. Forster

15. *The Civil War*, Shelby Foote

16. *The Guns of August*, Barbara Tuchman

17. *The Proper Study of Mankind*, Isaiah Berlin

18. *The Nature and Destiny of Man*, Reinhold Niebuhr

19. *Notes of a Native Son*, James Baldwin

20. *The Autobiography of Alice B. Toklas*, Gertrude Stein

21. *The Elements of Style*, William Strunk & E. B. White

22. *An American Dilemma*, Gunnar Myrdal

23. *Principia Mathematica*, Alfred North Whitehead & Bertrand Russell

24. *The Mismeasure of Man*, Jay Stephen Gould

25. *The Mirror and the Lamp*, Meyer Howard Abrams

26. *The Art of the Soluble*, Peter B. Medawar

27. *The Ants*, Bert Hoelldobler & Edward O. Wilson

28. *A Theory of Justice*, John A. Rawls

29. *Art and Illusion*, Ernest H. Gombrich

30. *The Making of the English Working Class*, E. P. Thompson

31. *The Souls of Black Folk*, W. E. B. Du Bois

32. *Principia Ethica*, G. E. Moore

33. *Philosophy and Civilization*, John Dewey

34. *On Growth and Form*, D'Arcy Thompson

35. *Ideas and Opinions*, Albert Einstein

36. *The Age of Jackson*, Arthur Schlesinger, Jr.

37. *The Making of the Atomic Bomb*, Richard Rhodes

38. *Black Lamb and Grey Falcons*, Rebecca West

39. *Autobiographies*, W. B. Yeats

40. *Science and Civilization in China*, Joseph Needham

41. *Goodbye to All That*, Robert Graves

42. *Homage to Catalonia*, George Orwell

43. *The Autobiography of Mark Twain*, Mark Twain

44. *Children of Crisis*, Robert Coles

45. *A Study of History*, Arnold J. Toynbee

46. *The Affluent Society*, John Kenneth Galbraith

47. *Present at the Creation*, Dean Acheson

48. *The Great Bridge*, David McCullough

49. *Patriotic Gore*, Edmund Wilson

50. *Samuel Johnson*, Walter Johnson Bate

51. *The Autobiography of Malcolm X*, Alex Haley & Malcolm X

52. *The Right Stuff*, Tom Wolfe

53. *Eminent Victorians*, Lytton Strachey

54. *Working*, Studs Terkel

55. *Darkness Visible*, William Styron

56. *The Liberal Imagination*, Lionel Trilling

57. *The Second World War*, Winston Churchill

58. *Out of Africa*, Isak Dinesen

59. *Jefferson and His Time*, Dumas Malone

60. *In the American Grain*, William Carlos Williams

61. *Cadillac Desert*, Marc Reisner

62. *The House of Morgan*, Ron Chernow

63. *The Sweet Science*, A. J. Liebling

64. *The Open Society and Its Enemies*, Karl Popper

65. *The Art of Memory*, Frances A. Yates

66. *H. Religion and the Rise of Capitalism*, R. H. Tawney

67. *A Preface to Morals*, Walter Lippmann

68. *The Gate of Heavenly Peace*, Jonathan D. Spence

69. *The Structure of Scientific Revolutions*, Thomas S. Kuhn

70. *The Strange Career of Jim Crow*, C. Vann Woodward

71. *The Rise of the West*, William H. McNeill

72. *The Gnostic Gospels,* Elaine Pagels

73. *James Joyce,* Richard Ellmann

74. *Florence Nightingale,* Cecil Woodham-Smith

75. *The Great War and Modern Memory,* Paul Fussell

76. *The City in History,* Lewis Mumford

77. *Battle Cry of Freedom,* James M. McPherson

78. *Why We Can't Wait,* Martin Luther King, Jr.

79. *The Rise of Theodore Roosevelt,* Edmund Morris

80. *Studies in Iconology,* Erwin Panofsky

81. *The Face of Battle,* John Keegan

82. *The Strange Death of Liberal England,* George Dangerfield

83. *Vermeer,* Lawrence Gowing

84. *A Bright Shining Lie,* Neil Sheehan

85. *West with the Night,* Beryl Markham

86. *This Boy's Life,* Tobias Wolff

87. *A Mathematician's Apology,* G. H. Hardy

88. *Six Easy Pieces,* Richard P. Feynman

89. *Pilgrim at Tinker Creek,* Annie Dillard

90. *The Golden Bough,* James George Frazer

91. *Shadow and Act,* Ralph Ellison

92. *The Power Broker,* Robert A. Caro

93. *The American Political Tradition*, Richard Hofstadter

94. *The Contours of American History*, William Appleman Williams

95. *The Promise of American Life*, Herbert Croly

96. *In Cold Blood*, Truman Capote

97. *The Journalist and the Murderer*, Janet Malcolm

98. *The Taming of Chance*, Ian Hacking

99. *Operating Instructions*, Anne Lamott

100. *Melbourne*, Lord David Cecil

Fiction

1. *Ulysses*, James Joyce

2. *The Great Gatsby*, F. Scott Fitzgerald

3. *A Portrait of the Artist As a Young Man*, James Joyce

4. *Lolita*, Vladimir Nabokov

5. *Brave New World*, Aldous Huxley

6. *The Sound and The Fury*, William Faulkner

7. *Catch-22*, Joseph Heller

8. *Darkness at Noon*, Arthur Koestler

9. *Sons and Lovers*, D. H. Lawrence

10. *The Grapes of Wrath*, John Steinbeck

11. *Under the Volcano*, Malcolm Lowry

12. *The Way of All Flesh*, Samuel Butler

13. *1984*, George Orwell

14. I, *Claudius*, Robert Graves

15. *To the Lighthouse*, Virginia Woolf

16. *An American Tragedy*, Theodore Dreiser

17. *The Heart is a Lonely Hunter*, Carson McCullers

18. *Slaughterhouse-Five*, Kurt Vonnegut

19. *Invisible Man*, Ralph Ellison

20. *Native Son*, Richard Wright

21. *Henderson the Rain King*, Saul Bellow

22. *Appointment in Samarra*, John O'Hara

23. *U.S.A.* (trilogy), John Dos Passos

24. *Winesburg, Ohio*, Sherwood Anderson

25. *A Passage to India*, E. M. Forster

26. *The Wings of the Dove*, Henry James

27. *The Ambassadors*, Henry James

28. *Tender is the Night*, F. Scott Fitzgerald

29. *The Studs Lonigan Trilogy*, James T. Farrell

30. *The Good Soldier*, Ford Madox Ford

31. *Animal Farm*, George Orwell

32. *The Golden Bowl*, Henry James

33. *Sister Carrie*, Theodore Dreiser

34. *A Handful of Dust*, Evelyn Waugh

35. *As I Lay Dying*, William Faulkner

36. *All the King's Men*, Robert Penn Warren

37. *The Bridge of San Luis Rey*, Thornton Wilder

38. *Howards End*, E. M. Forster

39. *Go Tell It on the Mountain*, James Baldwin

40. *The Heart of the Matter*, Graham Greene

41. *Lord of the Flies*, William Golding

42. *Deliverance*, James Dickey

43. *A Dance to the Music of Time* (series), Anthony Powell

44. *Point Counter Point*, Aldous Huxley

45. *The Sun Also Rises*, Ernest Hemingway

46. *The Secret Agent*, Joseph Conrad

47. *Nostromo*, Joseph Conrad

48. *The Rainbow*, D. H. Lawrence

49. *Women in Love*, D.H. Lawrence

50. *Tropic of Cancer*, Henry Miller

51. *The Naked and the Dead*, Norman Mailer

52. *Portnoy's Complaint*, Philip Roth

53. *Pale Fire*, Vladimir Nabokov

54. *Light in August*, William Faulkner

55. *On the Road*, Jack Kerouac

56. *The Maltese Falcon*, Dashiell Hammett

57. *Parade's End*, Ford Madox Ford

58. *The Age of Innocence*, Edith Wharton

59. *Zuleika Dobson*, Max Beerbohm

60. *The Movie Goer*, Walker Percy

61. *Death Comes for the Archbishop*, Willa Cather

62. *From Here to Eternity*, James Jones

63. *The Wapshot Chronicles*, John Cheever

64. *The Catcher in the Rye*, J. D. Salinger

65. *A Clockwork Orange*, Anthony Burgess

66. *Of Human Bondage*, W. Somerset Maugham

67. *Heart of Darkness*, Joseph Conrad

68. *Main Street*, Sinclair Lewis

69. *The House of Mirth*, Edith Wharton

70. *The Alexandria Quartet*, Lawrence Durell

71. *A High Wind in Jamaica*, Richard Hughes

72. *A House for Mr. Biswas*, V. S. Naipaul

73. *The Day of the Locust*, Nathaniel West

74. *A Farewell to Arms*, Ernest Hemingway

75. *Scoop*, Evelyn Waugh

76. *The Prime of Miss Jean Brodie*, Muriel Spark

77. *Finnegans Wake*, James Joyce

78. *Kim*, Rudyard Kipling

79. *A Room with A View*, E. M. Forster

80. *Brideshead Revisited*, Evelyn Waugh

81. *The Adventures of Augie March*, Saul Bellow

82. *Angle of Repose*, Wallace Stegner

83. *A Bend in the River*, V. S. Naipaul

84. *The Death of the Heart*, Elizabeth Bowen

85. *Lord Jim*, Joseph Conrad

86. *Ragtime*, E. L. Doctorow

87. *The Old Wives' Tale*, Arnold Bennett

88. *The Call of the Wild*, Jack London

89. *Loving*, Henry Green

90. *Midnight's Children*, Salman Rushdie

91. *Tobacco Road*, Erskine Caldwell

92. *Ironweed*, William Kennedy

93. *The Magus*, John Fowles

94. *Wide Sargasso Sea*, Jean Rhys

95. *Under the Net*, Iris Murdoch

96. *Sophie's Choice*, William Styron

97. *The Sheltering Sky*, Paul Bowles

98. *The Postman Always Rings Twice*, James M. Cain

99. *The Ginger Man*, J. P. Donleavy

100. *The Magnificent Ambersons*, Booth Tarkington

Appendix D

Keep a Journal

Follow these guidelines to help you start a journal and keep it going.

- Emphasize thoughts and feeling rather than events. Write only enough of an event to spark your memory when, years from now, you reread your journal. What will grip you in ten years? No doubt it will be the moments that made you laugh or cry, or at least feel something. You won't be interested in what time you woke or what you had for breakfast. The coffee might have been great, but it's probably not worth writing about. On the other hand, if during breakfast your partner gave you a provocative look that sent your pulse racing, you might enjoy rediscovering that feeling. Similarly, if you gave an exhilarating PowerPoint presentation at work, you don't have to put down the details of the presentation itself; instead describe the reactions to it—who was encouraging, who was catty—including your own reactions.

- Don't feel you have to write down every movement or activity of the day. The most common complaint of journal writers is "I have nothing to write about," as if nothing "important" ever happens to them. But a journal is more than just a record of the daily events of one's life. A journal offers the opportunity to confront not just what happened to you but how you felt about it.

- As you write, give free rein to your creativity. Write descriptions, dialogues, rants, whatever. Use all your senses and writing skills to peel back not just your own emotions but those of others. This will sharpen your awareness of the subconscious.

- Consider dividing your journal into sections: Ideas for Pieces . . . Character Sketches . . . Pertinent Observations . . . Poems . . . and so on.

- Don't feel you have to write every day. The last thing you want is to make journaling a chore. If daily writing is unrealistic, shoot for twice a week, or even twice a month.

- Keep a pen and notebook by your bed. Jot notes, just enough to trigger thoughts when you sit down to write.

- Take chances. There are no sacred rules that can't be broken. One aim is to enable you to return to your journal someday and relive the highs and lows of your life. But the more immediate goal is to get you writing—regardless of what you write.

- Periodically mine your journal for ideas, images, and phrases that might be used in a piece you're working on.

Exercises

- What aren't you proud of? Compose a journal entry that begins "No one knows about the time that . . ."

- Write about something you wish someone would give you. What would your life be like if you were given this thing?

- Reread your entries. How would you characterize yourself from the readings? Show, don't tell. No judgment words allowed.

Appendix E

Master Basic Grammar

Although you can still be a creative writer if you tend to mix up "I" and "me," grammar problems can inhibit your creativity. It's like trying to be a sculptor without a chisel, knife, or paper maché. Think of grammar as the tools that allow you to build what you want.

On the other hand, poor command of English grammar can be a warning signal to editors that you lack professionalism and to all readers that you lack credibility or precision. Know your weak spots and work on them.

Here are a few of the most common grammatical/syntax errors that writers make:

- I/me/myself. In simplest terms, I is subject, me is object, and myself should almost never be used.

    John and I [not me] *went to the store.*
    Between you and me, Brad is a jerk.

    Use *myself* only for emphasis—*I myself would never do that*, or when it's reflexive—*I hit myself on the head with a hammer.*

- Like/as. Use *like* when comparing nouns and *as* when comparing verbs, or action. So, "Be like me," but "Do as I do."

- Further/farther. Though few people make the distinction anymore, *farther* applies to physical distance, *further* to degree or metaphorical distance. You travel farther, but pursue a topic further.

- Who/whom. Both who and whom are pronouns. If you can substitute "he" or "she," then *who* is correct; if you can substitute "him" or "her," then *whom* is correct. "Who was at the door?" (He was at the door.) "Whom did Ben see?" (Ben saw her.)

- Less/fewer. *Less* means "not as much"; *fewer* means "not as many." If you'd use *much*, it's *less*; if you'd use many, it's *fewer*. In other words, if you can count the items, use fewer. You have less mashed potatoes but fewer potatoes.

- Bad/badly. If your child falls down and skins her knee, you feel bad, not badly. Sensing that they are modifying the verb feel, more and more people use badly in that situation. But what you are really modifying is you the person, a noun. About the only time you feel badly is when you've had your fingertips erased.

- Lay/lie. *Lay* means to put something down, to place something. Its principal forms are lay, laid, (have) laid, and laying. "Ben *laid* the tools on the desk." "Where did I *lay* my books?" *Lie* means to rest or recline. Its principal forms are *lie, lay,* (have) *lain,* and *lying.* (Its past tense, *lay,* should not be confused with the verb *lay.*) "She likes to *lie* down after school." "Steph has *lain* in bed all day."

- It's/its. *It's* is a contraction for *it is*; so if you can't sensibly substitute it is, then *it's* is correct.

- Between/among. When two things or persons are involved, use *between*; with three or more, use *among*. "The jellybeans were divided *among* the four kids." "*Between* you and me, Bill has no chance."

- Disinterested/uninterested. *Disinterested* means impartial, as judges should be. An *uninterested* person is not interested.

- Affect/effect. Affect and effect are not synonyms. Affect is usually a verb. It means to sway, influence, or impress. "The loss of Mary's notes will *affect* her confidence." Effect can be either a noun or a verb. As a noun, effect means the result of some action. "The *effect* of installing the new lathe was an increase in production." As a verb, effect means to accomplish something. "The new president effected several changes."

- Unique. Because unique means one of a kind, there are no degrees of uniqueness. Something is either unique or it isn't. Don't use more or most to modify unique. Often the better choice is unusual.

- Literally/figuratively. Writers too often write *literally* when they mean *figuratively*. For example: "Catherine was literally blown out of his socks." Was Catherine separated from his socks? If not, the writer should delete literally.

- That/which. Use *that* to introduce a restrictive clause and *which* to introduce a nonrestrictive or parenthetical one. "Your manuscript is both good and original; but the part that is good is not original, and the part that is original is not good." "My decision, which did not come easily, is final."

- Whose/who's. *Who's* is a contraction of *who is*. *Whose* is the possessive. Thus: "Who's the idiot whose Cadillac is blocking the driveway?"

- Principle/principal. Most of us remember that the *principal* of the school is our "pal." But principal can also be an adjective meaning "first" or "most important." "The principal told the students the principal rule was to play by the rules." Principal can also be a noun meaning "a sum of money." On the other hand, *principle* is a noun meaning "a basic truth or law." Thus: "Martin Luther King, Jr. was a man of unwavering principles."

- Should've/should of. Because the spoken word tends to be sloppy, people say *should of* when they mean *should have*. Unless they are doing dialect, writers must be more precise. Should have, or its contraction *should've* is correct.

- Every is/are. *Each* and *every* take singular verbs. So when a national tutoring service advertised that "*Every* parent wants their child to succeed in school," it is not a good testimonial to their ability to teach English skills. What are the options? First choice is often to make the sentence plural: "All parents want their children to succeed." But sometimes the plural is unwieldy or off target. If so, the quality of the choices diminishes. You can substitute *his* for *their*, but that's sexist language. You can try *his* or *her* or the clunky *his/her*. Another possibility: alternate throughout the piece between *his* and *her*.

Other Grammar Pitfalls

- Watch out for flabby modifiers. Modifiers that say nothing, such as *absolutely, really, truly, just,* and the dreaded *very,* should be used rarely or never.

- Look out for the preposition *of,* which is often an indication of wordy writing. For example: "She is the type *of* woman who can't be trusted." It's usually better to write, "She can't be trusted."

- Be careful when using *which is, who are,* and *who is.* They are frequently unnecessary. "The film, *which is* a mystery, takes place in Paris." Better: "The film, a mystery, takes place in Paris."

- Red flag any sentences that begin with *there is/are, it is,* or the like. It's a wordy construction. "There *are* four men drinking at the bar." Better: "Four men sat drinking at the bar."

Other Easily Confused Words

It isn't always easy to know which word to use. Do you spread jam or jelly on your toast? When you're sick, do you have a temperature or a fever? These words are similar but not synonymous. Here are a few more that people tend to confuse.

- Allusion vs. illusion. Allusion is a noun that means an indirect reference: "The speech made allusions to the final report." Illusion is a noun that means a misconception: "The policy is designed to give an illusion of reform."

- Bimonthly vs. semimonthly. Bimonthly is an adjective that means every two months: "I brought the cake for the bimonthly office party." Bimonthly is also a noun that means a publication issued every two months: "The bimonthly [magazine] will soon become a monthly publication." Semimonthly is an adjective that means happening twice a month: "We have semimonthly meetings on the 1st and the 15th."

- Cite vs. site. Cite is a verb that means to quote as an authority or example: "I cited several eminent scholars in my study of water resources." It also means to recognize formally: "The public official was cited for service to the city." It can also mean to summon before a court of law: "Last year the company was cited for pollution violations."

Site is a noun meaning location: "They chose a new site for the factory just outside town."

- Complement vs. compliment. Complement is a noun or verb that means something that completes or makes up a whole: "The red sweater is a perfect complement to the outfit." Compliment is a noun or verb that means an expression of praise or admiration: "I received many compliments about my new outfit."

- Concurrent vs. consecutive. Concurrent is an adjective that means simultaneous or happening at the same time as something else: "The concurrent strikes of several unions crippled the economy." Consecutive means successive or following one after the other: "The union called three consecutive strikes in one year."

- Connote vs. denote. Connote is a verb that means to imply or suggest: "The word 'espionage' connotes mystery and intrigue." Denote is a verb that means to indicate or refer to specifically: "The symbol for 'pi' denotes the number 3.14159."

- Discreet vs. discrete. Discreet is an adjective that means prudent, circumspect, or modest: "Their discreet comments about the negotiations led the reporters to expect an early settlement." Discrete is an adjective that means separate or individually distinct: "Each company in the conglomerate operates as a discrete entity."

- Stationary vs. stationery. Stationary, an adjective, means unmoving. "They maneuvered around the *stationary* barrier in the road." *Stationery* is a noun that means writing materials: "We printed the letters on company *stationery*."

Rules Worth Breaking

Sloppy grammar hinders your ability to communicate clearly. But you should not let strict adherence to the rules of grammar get in the way of good writing. Here are five grammatical "rules" you should feel free to break for the sake of lively writing.

1. Never use the same word twice in a sentence. More a rule of style than grammar, this has caused many a writer to reach for obscure synonyms that clutter sentences. You don't want your prose reading like

a thesaurus. In the following example, repeating the word "computer" would be preferable to stretching for alternatives.

The computer repairman opened the back of the machine and fiddled inside the gizmo until at last the electronic contraption's screen lit up and the digital thingamabob purred to life.

2. Don't end a sentence with a preposition. *Modern English Usage* calls this a "persistent myth." Winston Churchill once ridiculed a strict adherence to the rule by declaring, "This is the sort of English up with which I will not put." Avoid such gymnastics if ending a sentence with a preposition sounds better.

3. Don't use sentence fragments. Technically, every sentence must have a subject and a verb to qualify for a period. That said, using sentence fragments sparingly can add punch to your prose. Fragments underscore the thoughts you've packed into your terse, verbless phrases. Consider the following passage from Gore Vidal's historical novel *Burr*: "The American soldier was as mercenary as any Hessian. No money, no battle." This construction generates more power than, say, this: "If they weren't paid, they wouldn't fight."

4. Don't split infinitives. This rule prohibits placing a word between "to" and the accompanying verb. But sometimes splitting an infinitive can add needed emphasis. *Modern English Usage* offers this example by Garrison Keillor: "The only unforgivable sin is to not show up." Keillor adds weight to the word "not" by placing it between "to" and "show." When trying to decide whether or not to split, listen to how the sentence sounds and judge on that basis. In any case, don't let the avoidance of split infinitives make your writing wooden or awkward.

The Fumblerules of Grammar

For your amusement and education, here are "The Fumblerules of Grammar," by William Safire:

1. No sentence fragments.

2. Avoid run-on sentences they are hard to read.

3. Use the semicolon properly, always use it where it is appropriate; and never where it isn't.

4. If a dependent clause precedes an independent clause put a comma after the dependent clause.

5. Avoid commas, that are not necessary.

6. Reserve the apostrophe for it's proper use and omit it when its not needed.

7. Don't use contractions in formal writing.

8. Don't overuse exclamation points!!!

9. Unqualified superlatives are the worst of all.

10. In statements involving two word phrases, make an all out effort to use hyphens.

11. Verbs have to agree with their subjects.

12. Remember to never split an infinitive.

13. If any word is improper at the end of a sentence, a linking verb is.

14. The passive voice should never be used.

15. Write all adverbial forms correct.

16. Writing carefully, dangling participles must be avoided.

17. Never, ever use repetitive redundancies.

18. If you reread your work, you will find on rereading that a great deal of repetition can be avoided by rereading and editing.

19. Never use a long word when a diminutive one will do.

20. Don't string too many prepositional phrases together unless you are walking through the valley of the shadow of death.

21. Everyone should be careful to use a singular pronoun with singular nouns in their writing.

22. Place pronouns as close as possible, especially in long sentences, as of ten or more words, to their antecedents.

23. A writer must not shift your point of view.

24. Proofread carefully to see if you any words out.

Appendix F

Learn to Spell

The following guidelines focus on some of the most common spelling problems:

Suffixes

1. -ance or—ence.

    When the final c or g has a soft sound, use—ence,—ent, or—ency. For example: magnificent, emergency, indigent, obsolescence.

    When the final c or g has a hard sound, use—ance,—ant, or—ancy. For example: significant, extravagant.

2. -able or—ible

    Words that have an—ation form usually take—able. For example: dispensable (dispensation), quotable (quotation), irritable (irritation), imaginable (imagination).

    Words that have an—ive,—tion,—sion, or—id form usually take—ible. For example: combustible (combustion), reversible (reversion), collectible (collective), digestible (digestion). Exception: definable (definition).

3. -ceed,—cede, or—sede.

   Three English words end with—ceed: exceed, proceed, and succeed. One ends with—sede: supersede. All others ending in this syllable are spelled—cede. For example: accede, concede, precede, secede.

4. -ize or—ise

   This verb's suffix is often spelled—ize in the United States (ostracize, galvanize, pasteurize, sanitize) and—ise in Great Britain (ostracise). Even in the U.S., however, use—ise for the following words: advertise, chastise, exorcise, franchise.

Adding Suffixes

When a word ends in *ie*, replace it with *y*. For example: die, dying; lie, lying.

Prefixes

Prefixes added to the beginning of a base word change the meaning but not the spelling of the base word. Common prefixes, such as *un, mis, over,* and *under,* should not be hyphenated—as in *unmistakable, misunderstand, overstatement,* and *underworld.*

Spelling Rules

Memorizing rules is usually not the most effective way to learn spelling. Most rules have exceptions—and besides, you are best at learning words that you have made an effort to understand. A good way to understand a word is to break it into syllables. Look for prefixes, suffixes, and roots. Practice each short part and then the whole word. dis-ap-pear-ing tra-di-tion-al

After you break apart a word, ask yourself: How is this word like other words I know? Spelling the word traditional may make you think of how to spell functional and national. Finding patterns among words is one of the best ways to learn spelling.

1. Here are some common spelling rules that illustrate the limitations of memorization.

Learned as a childhood rhyme, this may be the best-known of the bunch:

i *before e, except after c or when sounded like "ay" as in neighbor and weigh*

Here are some words that follow the rule: *ie* words: believe, field, relief *cei* words: ceiling, deceit, receive *ei* words: freight, reign, sleigh
Some words that don't follow the rule: either, foreign, height, leisure, protein, weird.
Another category of exceptions: *cien* words, such as ancient, efficient, and science.

2. Here's another familiar spelling rule: "Silent *e* helps a vowel say its name." This means that when a word ends with a vowel followed by a consonant and then a silent *e*, the vowel has a long sound. That's the difference between rate and rat, hide and hid, and cube and cub.

3. Have you heard the expression "When two vowels go walking, the first one does the talking?" This means that when one vowel follows another, the first usually has a long sound and the second is silent. That's why it's team, not taem; coat, not caot; and wait, not wiat. Remembering this rule will help you to put vowels in the right order.

4. Learn the basic rules for spelling with plural nouns so that you know whether to use *s* or *es* and how to make plurals of nouns that end in *y* or *f*. Is it bullys or bullies?

5. It's also helpful to try making up a funny memory aids. For example, do you have trouble remembering which has a double s—desert (arid land) or dessert (a sweet treat)? Remember that with dessert, you'd like seconds. Or maybe you have trouble remembering how to spell separate? Remember that there's a rat in the middle.

6. Another kind of memory aid is to make up a sentence in which the first letter of each word can be used to make the spelling word. The sillier the better—goofy sentences may be easier to remember.

• chili: cats have interesting little ideas

• physical: please have your strawberry ice cream and lollipops

7. Make sure that you are pronouncing words correctly. This can help you to avoid some common spelling errors, such as *canidate* instead of *candidate*, *jewelery* instead of *jewelry*, and *libary* instead of *library*.

8. Put together a list of words that you find difficult to spell; now see if the tips above will help you.

9. Don't rely exclusively on electronic spellcheckers. They can miss errors—especially when you have used the wrong word but spelled it correctly. For example, a spellchecker would find no problems with either sentence below:

- "I might need some new shoes for gym," Harry told our Aunt Ann.

- "Eye mite knead sum knew shoos four Jim," Hairy tolled hour Ant an.

Common Words Easily Misspelled

Here is a partial list of common words that can be a challenge to spell. Add your own bugaboos to the list.

- accommodate
- accumulate
- acknowledgment
- acquaintance
- acquire
- aggravate
- all right
- amateur
- appetite
- business

- calendar
- cemetery
- committee
- concede
- conscientious
- conscious
- consensus
- correspondence
- definite
- dependent

- desirable
- despair
- desperate
- dining
- doctor
- eighth
- eligible
- embarrass
- exaggerated
- existence
- February
- foreign
- fulfill
- grammar
- grievous
- harass
- height
- illegible
- immigrant
- independent
- indispensable
- inoculate interfere

- iridescence
- irresistible
- judgment
- knowledge
- laboratory
- legible
- leisure
- liaison
- listen
- maneuver
- miscellaneous
- mischievous
- misspell
- mortgage
- necessary
- nickel
- ninety
- noticeable
- occasionally
- occurred
- occurrence
- outrageous

- parallel
- permissible
- perseverance
- possession
- precede
- preference
- preferred
- privilege
- prerogative
- procedure
- proceed
- professor
- prominent
- propeller
- quizzes
- recognize
- recommend
- reconnaissance
- referred
- renaissance
- restaurant
- rhythm

- schedule
- seize
- separate
- severely
- shining
- sophomore
- succeed
- superintendent
- syllable
- synonym
- temperament
- transferring
- twelfth
- undoubtedly
- unnecessary
- vegetable
- vengeance
- villain
- Wednesday
- weird
- wholly

Tough Words Correctly Spelled

The National Spelling Bee was launched by the Louisville *Courier-Journal* in 1925. Over the years the national finals have grown from a mere 9 contestants to about 250. In 2003, 13-year-old Dallas eighth-grader Sai Gunturi won $12,000 and other prizes for correctly spelling pococurante. Here are the deciding words the past few years:

1979: maculature	1994: antediluvian
1980: elucubrate	1995: xanthosis
1981: sarcophagus	1996: vivisepulture
1982: psoriasis	1997: euonym
1983: Purim	1998: chiaroscurist
1984: luge	1999: logorrhea
1985: milieu	2000: demarche
1986: odontalgia	2001: succedaneum
1987: staphylococci	2002: prospicience
1988: elegiacal	2003: pococurante
1989: spoliator	2004: autochthonous
1990: fibranne	2005: appoggiatura
1991: antipyretic	2006: ursprache
1992: lyceum	2007: serrefine
1993: kamikaze	2008: querdon

Appendix G

Simplicity

William Zinsser's essay "Simplicity" is the best I've read on the importance of writing with clarity. Here's an excerpt from his classic guide to writing nonfiction, *On Writing Well*:

> *Clutter is the disease of American writing. We are a society strangling in unnecessary words, circular constructions, pompous frills and meaningless jargon.*
>
> *Who can understand the viscous language of everyday American commerce and enterprise: the business letter, the interoffice memo, the corporation report, the notice from the bank explaining its latest "simplified" statement? What member of an insurance or medical plan can decipher the brochure that describes what the costs and benefits are? What father or mother can put together a child's toy—on Christmas Eve or any other eve—from the instructions on the box?*
>
> *Our national tendency is to inflate and thereby sound important. The airline pilot who announces that he is presently anticipating experiencing considerable precipitation wouldn't dream of saying that it may rain. The sentence is too simple—there must be something wrong with it.*
>
> *But the secret of good writing is to strip every sentence to its cleanest components.*

Every word that serves no function, every long word that could be a short word, every adverb that carries the same meaning that's already in the verb, every passive construction that leaves the reader unsure of who is doing what—these are the thousand and one adulterants that weaken the strength of a sentence. And they usually occur, ironically, in proportion to education and rank.

It's not just politicians and attorneys who engage in cluttered obfuscation. Thanks to the Plain English Campaign, we can make fun of this breathtaking 102-word sentence put out by the Association of Chief Police Officers.

The promise of reform which the Green Paper heralds holds much for the public and Service alike; local policing, customized to local need with authentic answerability, strengthened accountabilities at force level through reforms to Police Authorities and HMIC, performance management at the service of localities with targets and plans tailored to local needs, the end of centrally engineered one size fits all initiatives, an intelligent approach to cutting red tape through redesign of processes and cultures, a renewed emphasis on strategic development so as to better equip our Service to meet the amorphous challenges of managing cross force harms, risks and opportunities.

Marie Clair, spokeswoman for Plain English Campaign, compares reading this sentence to wrestling with a jellyfish, then makes this larger point: "This is not the example we need from the top. There's nothing but confusion and mistrust in using jargon when plain English will do."

At the other end of the clarity spectrum, here's a famous passage from Henry David Thoreau's memoir, *Walden*. Note the power he generates from simple language.

I went to the woods because I wished to live deliberately, to front only the essential facts of life, and see if I could not learn what it had to teach, and not, when I came to die, discover that I had not lived. I did not wish to live what was not life, living is so dear; nor did I wish to practice resignation, unless it was quite necessary. I wanted to live deep and suck out all the marrow of life, to live so sturdily and Spartan-like as to put to rout all that was not life, to cut a broad swath and shave close, to drive life into a corner, and reduce it to its lowest terms, and, if it proved to be mean, why then to get the whole and genuine meanness of it, and publish its meanness to the world; or if it were sublime, to know it by experience, and be able to give a true account of it.

Clear writing begins with clear thinking. If your thinking is murky, your writing will reflect that. And you will lose your reader, maybe not in the first sentence, but soon.

Zinsser characterizes the reader as "someone with an attention span of about sixty seconds—a person assailed by forces competing for the minutes that might otherwise be spent on a magazine or a book . . . The person snoozing in a chair, holding a magazine or a book, is a person who was being given too much unnecessary trouble by the writer."

Before you write, ask yourself: What am I trying to say? As you write, continue to ask that question. When you finish the first draft, look at what you've written and ask: Have I said it? Imagine it from the point of view of someone confronting this subject for the first time.

Zinsser rejects the notion that some people are naturally Clear Thinkers and others Muddled Thinkers. "Thinking clearly is a conscious act that writers must force upon themselves, just as if they were embarking on any other project that requires logic: adding up a laundry list or doing an algebra problem. Good writing doesn't come naturally, though most people obviously think it does. The professional writer is constantly being bearded by strangers who say they'd like to 'try a little writing sometime'—meaning when they retire from their real profession, like insurance or real estate. Or they say, 'I could write a book about that.' I doubt it."

Finally, Zinsser leaves us with hope and a recipe for success: "Writing is hard work. A clear sentence is no accident. Very few sentences come out right the first time, or even the third time. Remember this as a consolation in moments of despair. If you find that writing is hard, it's because it is hard. It's one of the hardest things that people do."

Appendix H

Craft Gripping Leads

The samples below, which focus on how to study effectively for tests, reflect four typical approaches to writing leads—question, quote, general, and specific. Compare the four and decide which you prefer. Which would make you want to read on? Why? Discuss it with others.

- Lead 1: Jackson is a typical high school junior. Last night he was studying for a major history test. Feeling that music relaxes him, he put on the stereo and hit the books. After two hours—during which he treated himself to some snacks and his favorite TV show—he decided that he had studied enough. After all, he had put in two hours. The next day Jason bombed. Why? He doesn't know how to study for tests.

- Lead 2: "Students fail tests because they don't know how to study," says Ed Harmon, a high school history teacher. Harmon's statement is echoed by teachers throughout the country.

- Lead 3: Do you know how to study for tests? If you answered yes, you are in the minority. Most students don't know how to study for tests effectively.

- Lead 4: Test-taking is a major activity in American schools. It is also one of the most anxiety-causing. The reason for this comes down to a simple fact—most students don't know how to study for tests.

Examples

Writers who want to begin at the beginning often pen these words "I was born . . ." It seems logical, but there is no shortage of alternatives to add spice to the opening.

Recently I asked my writing students to start their autobiography two different ways, one of which had to begin: "I was born . . ." Compare their two versions below and decide which you prefer.

Chuck 1: "I was born in the winter of 1934. It was too cold to snow that day. My mother knew this was the day. My father didn't. He was in the far corner of the reservation doing something with "talking wires" (telephone wires). He missed my first day in South Dakota."

Chuck 2: "My mother sailed from Scotland on the *S.S. Transylvania* in 1928. Times were tough worldwide, but her father found a job sheepherding in eastern Montana. My mother and father met in the cowboy town of Miles City, fell in love, and married. He took her to where his family had always lived, even before the stone people, to an Indian reservation in the middle of nowhere."

Yvonne 1: "I was born over the objections of my father. The doctor suggested that my mother was too frail to carry through another pregnancy, and it must have scared my father to death to think he may be left with five children to cope with on his own."

Yvonne 2: "World War II was eleven months old, and the British people—and surely the Germans, too—were beginning to realize that this conflict would not be over quickly. It was not an auspicious time for a family to add a sixth child. We were not poor—my first memories were of sparseness rather than poverty, a crucial difference of degree."

Wilma 1: "I was born on May 28, 1924, the first child of Kenneth and Verna Boggs. Since I was a girl, they named me Wilma May instead of William . . ."

Wilma 2: "My, what a complex life I've had these past eighty years. I hope my children, grandchildren, and great grandchildren will treasure my existence enough to open the pages of my autobiography from time to time. I say 'autobiography,' but that's too grandiose. I'm writing snippets, little stories, that reveal me."

Maudie 1: "I was born at Madison General Hospital on April 5, 1928, which makes me an Aries."

Maudie 2: "I write this for my daughter Katie, who is as interested in autobiography as I, to furnish background of her parents and of the people—aunts, uncles, cousins—who are related to her and she to them by blood and marriage. This information dates back to the first third of the 19th century when my great grandfather moved from Massachusetts to Michigan to Ohio and settled in Huntsberg, only to die there, along with his wife—reasons unknown—leaving their four-year-old son in the care of his stepmother, who packed up the boy and his belongings and drove by horse and carriage all the way east from Ohio to the Berkshires, where she left him with his Uncle John."

Exercises

- Create your own gripping lead, complete with active verbs and human interest. Make the reader need to read on.

- Look at the leads from some off your favorite books. Look critically at what works and what doesn't—and note why.

As a start, here are some notable leads:

Growing Up in New Guinea, by Margaret Mead

To the Manus native the world is a great platter, curving upwards on all sides, from his flat lagoon village where the pile-houses stand like long-legged birds, placid and unstirred by the changing tides.

The Feminine Mystique, by Betty Friedan

The problem lay buried, unspoken, for many years in the minds of American women.

History of the English-Speaking Peoples, by Winston Churchill

In the summer of the Roman year 699, now described as the year 55 before the birth of Christ, the Proconsul of Gaul, Gaius Julius Caesar, turned his gaze upon Britain.

The Right Stuff, by Tom Wolfe

Within five minutes, or ten minutes, no more than that, three of the others had called her on the telephone to ask her if she had heard that something had happened out there.

The Bible

In the beginning God created heaven and earth.

Baby and Child Care, by Benjamin Spock

You know more than you think you do.

Appendix I

Be a Storyteller

Read the short memoir below and note the storytelling techniques author Chuck Kensler uses.

French Nose

It was 1945 and I met a kid named James LeCompt. His black hair shone like a raven's wing. and he had perfect white teeth.

He was a new kid in our fifth-grade class until he stopped coming a week or two later. He was Sioux and kind of squeezed his words through his nose, like Sioux people do. My dad called it "French nose."

James and I ate lunch together on an old carved-up outdoor table near the school playground. We both had our lunches in paper sacks. He had a sandwich and I had a sandwich. Mine was peanut butter and jelly. Mom made it. and I had an apple and cupcake, too. He had a baloney, Miracle Whip, and white-bread sandwich. He made it. He said he made three of them every morning—the other two were for his brother and sister. He also had a chocolate Hostess cupcake. I guess his brother and sister had cupcakes, too. I traded him half of my peanut butter and jelly, and he tore his sandwich in half and shared it with me.

One day, James said, "We are going to Seattle pretty soon. Dad has a new job waiting for him. He knows how to weld together fighter planes for the war."

"Oh yeah?" squeaked out of me. I wondered why dads have to move when they get a new job. Criminy, it just didn't seem fair.

Then for some unknown reason I blurted out, "Hey! maybe our dads know each other. My dad helped build airfields so planes have a place to land. He worked on a secret airbase in Oregon last year. I'd tell you about it, but it's a military secret."

James, his brother, sister, and dad lived in a Buick. They had traveled from South Dakota to Washington state in the Buick and slept in it at night. Their dad would work somewhere during the day, and then they would meet and have a baloney-sandwich supper. and the next morning they would have a baloney-sandwich breakfast. If their dad picked cherries, peaches, or apples, then they would have some fruit with their baloney sandwiches.

He never mentioned his mother.

One day he was gone.

Years later we met again. His raven-wing hair had changed to drifted snow. He was a professor. He could speak Sioux words through his French nose. He said he still eats baloney sandwiches.

I never asked him about his mother.

Exercises

- Start your next story with the word *one*, as in: "One day, I . . ." That will put you "in the moment" and help you avoid generalities.

- Continue the stories started below, using only dialogue and a little stage movement.

1. He saw the answer key to the history test on the floor. It must have fallen out of Mrs. Thompson's book. No one was around. He needed an "A" on the test tomorrow . . .

2. It was dark by the time she left school. She did not like walking home alone like this, but she had no choice. She walked quickly, being careful to stay away from shadows. The sound startled her . . .

3. Anne had insulted her for the last time. She resolved to have it out with her once and for all. After all, the friendship had been shaky ever since the "Jeff" incident. Suddenly the phone rang . . .

Appendix J

Mix in Dialogue

Example 1

Read the following memoir by Louise Clark and note how she uses dialogue to advance the story and develop character. How would the story have suffered if the narrator had told the whole story, with no dialogue?

The Invasion

"Anna, would you please come here a minute?"

Hearing her mother call, Annalise reluctantly put down her book and ran to the kitchen. Linda slid a casserole into the oven, carefully closed the door and pulled her oven mitts off. She looked down at eleven-year-old Annalise, the girl she called "Amy, little chocolate girl," because she had the long, brown wavy hair and milk-chocolate eyes, inherited from her El Salvadorian great-grandmother. Although Annalise had hated to stop reading, her eyes had that sparkle that seemed to say, "I hope there's a good joke coming—I'm ready."

Linda smiled down at Annalise. "Honey, would you please watch over the boys while I run down to the library? Christine isn't here, Alec's asleep, and Clark is reading about outer space, so he won't even know I've gone. Just be here if Alec wakes up, and don't let Clark go outside until I get back. Our books are due, and the library closes soon. I shouldn't be gone more than fifteen minutes."

"Sure, Mom. Everything'll be OK," she said, anxious to get back to her book.

Linda gathered the big stack of books, put them in a box, and carried them to her car. Anna watched her mother drive away, then ran back to her book. She had just removed the bookmark and opened the book when she heard a peculiar sound coming from the back of the house. She went into her bedroom and peeked out. She saw, emerging from behind the neighbor's house, a group of men dressed in army camouflage, carrying rifles and walkie-talkies. Their heads were covered with black hoods, with only the eyes cut out.

Anna jerked away from the window and stood panting, her back against the wall. Her hands started to shake, and tears began to stream down her cheeks. She didn't know what to do. She moved to another window and peeked out again. Now there were more men—and they were slowly advancing toward her house, talking into the walkie-talkies and pointing their guns in her general direction.

Suddenly she heard some of the men pulling at the locked doors, trying to get in. It occurred to her that she had been reading a Baby Sitter's Club book, in which girls her age met danger and solved crimes. In a flash she realized that danger was more fun to read about than to experience. Panic threatened to overwhelm her, but she kept coming back to one thought: She had to protect her little brothers.

She took a deep breath, then, with new resolve, crept into the boys' room, and woke Clark. "Clark," she whispered, "crawl under your bed, way back into the corner, and don't move until I tell you to." Clark, seeing the tears running down her cheeks, stifled his natural curiosity and did as he was told. Anna gently shook Alec. When he opened his eyes, she said, "Alec, come with me. We're going into my bedroom." Alec listlessly opened his eyes and followed her into her room, like a robot.

When Anna looked out the window this time, she saw more men surrounding the house. One of them was talking into a walkie-talkie and gesturing with his rifle for the others to follow him. They were heading right for them!

Anna hugged Alec, and they both crawled under her bed, up against the wall. She whispered to Clark, "Don't make any noise, no matter what you do!" Then she pulled Alec close, patting his head. From their hiding place, they could still hear the men's voices and the sound of the doors shaking. Trembling, Anna thought she had never been so afraid in her life.

Meanwhile, in town, Linda returned her books and checked out one that Annalise had reserved. As she drove into the garage, she noticed someone running toward the neighbor's house. She dismissed it as some neighbor kid taking a shortcut through her yard. She unlocked the back door and walked into the kitchen, expecting the usual barrage of questions: "Mama, can I play outside?" "Mommy, can Tiffany come over?" "Mom, can I ride my bike?" But there was only silence, and that worried her. As she hurried along the hallway toward the bedrooms, she heard sniffling, then some muffled cries. Meanwhile, Anna had her hand over Alec's mouth. As soon as he'd heard his mother's voice, he had wanted to cry out and run to Linda. It took all of Annalise's strength to hold him. When their mother came in the room, the children all cried out as one, as if a dam had broken allowing torrential waters to rush through.

With her heart pounding in her ears, Linda cried out, "What is it? What happened?"

All three children whimpered, "Outside! Outside!"

"What about outside?"

"Men! Lots of men!" Annalise sobbed.

"They were coming to get us!" Clark croaked.

"Wif guns!!" Alec declared, with a trace of pride.

"What are you talking about?" Linda gathered everyone around her on the couch. "Annalise, you tell me. Is this a joke?"

Anna told the story between sobs. "S-s-s-oldiers were coming t-t-to our house. They were h-h-hiding behind Johnson's house, and coming toward us, and, and shaking our doors."

"They had black things on their heads and faces with only the eyes cut out!" Clark put in.

"Dey had guns, too, Mommy," Alec added.

"I don't understand," Linda said. "Where did they go?"

"We don't know," Clark whimpered.

"We stayed under our beds and tried not to make noise," Anna explained. "They couldn't get in, so they left."

"It was scawy." Alec whispered in her ear and hugged her closer. Their sobs eventually diminished.

A while later, Tom returned from work. When he had heard the story, he said, "I'll call the neighbors and see if they saw anything."

The children crowded on and around Linda and listened to Tom's voice from the next room. "I think that might be a good idea," he was saying. "We'll be here." He hung up and came into the room where his family greeted him with questioning looks.

"The Dorans are coming over to tell us what happened," Tom said.

A few moments later, the Dorans and their oldest boy were at the door.

The parents looked concerned. The son, dressed in camouflage shirt and pants, looked at the floor and fidgeted.

Once they were seated, the father said, "I think you'd better explain, Josh."

Josh began, "I'm, like, taking a class at school about movie making, ya know, and my friends and I were filming this afternoon. It was a war movie."

"Why didn't you tell someone what you were doing?" Mr. Doran said, his voice rising to the level of a town crier.

Looking back down at his feet, Josh muttered, "We saw the car leave and thought nobody was home. We wanted to finish before it got dark."

His father snorted with disgust. "You think that makes it OK? You scared these kids to tears. You knew that small children live here!"

"You should have called," Mrs. Doran said in a quiet voice intended to balance her husband's shouts.

Tom, relieved, said, "Well, it was certainly a mistake, but we're glad it wasn't a real invasion."

"Please call next time so we'll know when to expect the next attack," Linda added.

Josh nodded sheepishly, the parents apologized some more, and the Dorans left.

A few months later, Linda, Tom, and family moved to Orlando, Florida, which has not been invaded in centuries—unless you count the Pirates of the Caribbean.

Example 2

Dialogue should sound conversational. Giving characters long monologues without interruption is a common pitfall. In most real-world conversations, the snatches of conversation are short.

Consider this selection, Act I, Scene I, from Shakespeare's *Macbeth*:

A desert heath. Thunder and lightning. Enter three witches.

First Witch. When shall we three meet again? In thunder, lightning, or in rain?
Sec. Witch. When the hurlyburly's done, When the battle's lost and won.
Third Witch. That will be ere the set of sun.
First Witch. Where the place?
Sec. Witch. Upon the heath.
Third Witch. There to meet with Macbeth.
First Witch. I come, Graymalkin!
Sec. Witch. Paddock calls.
Third Witch. Anon.
All. Fair is foul, and foul is fair:

Hover through the fog and filthy air.
Exit.

Exercise

Consider the following setup: A boss of security guards is trying to exercise authority over a defiant employee. How would you sketch out those two characters using dialogue only? Here's one of many possibilities:

"Why aren't you wearing a necktie?" he asked.
"You don't need them with the summer uniforms."
"You're not wearing a summer uniform. You're wearing a winter uniform. Ties are regulation with the winter uniform."
"The only reason I'm wearing a winter uniform is that they were out of summer uniforms. It's a substitute."
"Look, I don't make the rules. I just enforce them. If you wear a winter uniform, you must wear a necktie. It's as simple as that. If I make an exception for you, everybody will want to dress like a slob in here, and I won't have that . . ."

Appendix K

Pique the Senses

Exercise

Select a place where you can observe something. You might consider a park, a baseball game, a restaurant, or your backyard. Observe the details of the place and record how your senses are stimulated.

Sight
_____

Touch
_____

Hearing
_____

Smell
_____

Taste
_____

Appendix L

Reveal Your Characters

You don't want to write about Mankind—leave that to the social scientists. Instead, write about Uncle Tim, who lost his toe in Korea; or Aunt Martha, an immigrant who passed through Ellis Island. Don't write about war, write about a soldier—or a soldier's wife. Readers need specific characters they can identify with, people who share some of their own problems and irritations, successes and failures.

Character Tips

1. Learn about people by observation. Listen to their speech patterns, watch their mannerisms.

2. Ask questions about each of your characters:

   - How would her best friend describe her?

   - What would her worst enemy's reaction be?

   - How would she see and rationalize herself? Does she see herself as clever, kind, short-tempered, timid, aggressive?

   - What do people like or dislike about her? Do they admire her, pity her, fear her?

   - Does she feel superior to others? Inferior?

Note: The traits elicited by those questions are abstract and general. Behavior is concrete and specific. So the next question is, what does the character do to demonstrate those traits in action?

3. Help us understand what your characters care about. This is the core of character. The goal can be cataclysmic or trivial, global or local. It may be money or world peace or a grade on a test. What matters is that the character cares about it. Whenever possible, show your character in a situation that challenges the part of him that cares and threatens something he considers important. Coax the reader to ask: "How would I feel in his place?"

4. Be specific. Readers want to meet a specific character in a specific setting. So don't talk about how you and the gang would (conditional tense) hang out on the streets of Chicago. Show us one particular day—say, that sticky summer day in 1932 when you got hit in the head with a stickball bat and . . .

5. Consider how much physical description to include. Wordsmiths like Conrad and Hawthorne, writing before the widespread use of cameras, described characters in elaborate detail. Contemporary writers use lighter strokes. If you provide less physical description, you invite readers to use their imaginations to fill gaps.

6. Weave description into action. Instead of saying Karen had shifty eyes, show Karen shifting her eyes in reaction to something. Use a habit or characteristic that strikes a distinctive note—chewing on an unlit cigar, Fu Manchu mustache, drooping eyelid, mismatched socks—and repeat as necessary. Show meaningful mannerisms—for example, George Raft, playing the coin-flipping gangster Guino Rinaldo in the movie *Scarface*.

7. Reveal character in various ways. Describe traits subjectively or objectively, or use a combination. Present characters through the narrator's eyes, through other characters' eyes, or both. Show them indirectly in terms of how they influence or relate to others.

8. Create a powerful introduction. Your characters must strike us from the get-go—in the way you, the writer, want us to be struck. First impressions of people are mostly emotional, something we sense before we think much about it. Think of your own first impressions of people. Consider appearance, handshake, first words, eye contact, and mannerisms.

Here are some ways to introduce a character:

- Description, appearance. *The hair was what you noticed. It was bright orange and stacked on top of her head in what they used to call a beehive.*

- Action. *The man lurched back into the shadows, one foot scraping on the pavement as if he couldn't lift his leg.*

- Thoughts, introspection. *Reggie pondered, scanning the passersby and trying to identify the person called X. A man, surely—or was it? The note gave no hint.*

- Dialogue.

  "Lookin' for someone?"

  Alice turned. A woman was standing in the doorway, an old woman a head shorter than she, with pinched features and squinty eyes. "Who are you?" she gulped.

  "Me? Depends on who you are, what you want."

9. Be a caricaturist. We don't remember first impressions as catalogued details. We don't recall each item of clothing, each mannerism. As writers, we emphasize particular qualities so that readers recognize the character from these alone. In writing, as in caricatures, the aim is to delineate in a few sharp strokes the essential ingredients of an impression. If, say, you were moved by the endearing way your spouse absentmindedly twirled her hair around her fingers, then revealing that habit may recreate that feeling for your reader.

Note how one or two brief symbolic physical details can stand for the character of someone. Describe an old woman as unsmiling with her nose angled toward the sky, and our picture is of uptight arrogance.

10. Reveal your characters through action. Bring your characters on stage and show them in action. "You are what you do," someone said, which is consistent with Aristotle's principle: "Character is revealed by action." Never say a character is irritating; show her popping her gum loudly or doing something else recognizably irritating.

Picture a woman waiting impatiently for a bus. How does she act? Maybe she cranes her neck and looks down the road. Or looks at her watch, paces, consults the timetable, taps her feet. Maybe she sits stoically, smoking a cigarette. She might try to read a magazine, glancing up frequently with an annoyed look on her face.

What about you, or Uncle Jay, or Aunt Minnie? Are they the type to wait 1) patiently, 2) nervously, 3) tensely, or 4) otherwise? Combine an action here, a mannerism there into a consistent pattern.

11. Keep your characters moving by pointing them toward their own private futures. You do that by giving them appropriate direction, goal, drive, and attitude.

    • Direction could be called your character's road to happiness. Consider the key human motivators, such as desire for power, adventure, security, recognition, and affection.

    • Goals are more specific than direction; they are borne of your character's dissatisfaction with the present situation.

    • Drive is the inner pressure, the intensity with which a character wants to change or reshape his situation. At its core: motivation. The end product of drive is attainment of a goal, so it's critical to know how important that goal is to your character. To what extremes is she willing to go to attain it?

    • Attitude is a character's feeling about some situation or subject. In other words, it's a hangup that's hard to shake. Attitude is a product or mix of heredity and environment, life's circumstances. A nun has one attitude toward men; a teenager quite another.

12. Don't let your people waste motion, unless it somehow advances the story or develops character. For example, don't have Uncle Buford engaged in idle sloth unless you're trying to portray him as a couch potato.

13. Show us multidimensional characters. Give the reader a sense that they have an inner life stirring beneath the surface. In the past, it was popular to create stock characters, based on an outstanding character trait. And so a glutton was always gluttonous, a philosopher always philosophical, and a bad guy was never good.

This is easier for a writer because one-dimensional characters never step out of their roles; they never complicate matters by being individuals; they never surprise us.

Realistic characters, on the other hand, are a mix of contradictions. The TV character Murphy Brown was attractive, intelligent, successful, but also aggressively opinionated and a recovering alcoholic. Or consider George Castanza on "Seinfeld," who was likeable despite copious flaws. To convince readers of their multidimensional nature, show characters not only by what they do and say, but by how they affect others.

14. Bring characters to life through dialogue. What Aunt Minnie says is important, but so is how she says it: the circumstances or context, the timing, and the cadence or pattern of speech. Repetition of phrases may help the reader recognize her. Pet expressions such as "righto" and "hell's bells" will help distinguish one character from another. So will accents, though they can be taxing on the reader. Certain vocations have their own cant, such as cops calling bad guys "perps."

    Inexperienced writers tend to let characters ramble on too long. Speech tends to be short, choppy, and full of interruptions.

    The same principle applies to talk as to action. Does it 1) reveal character? or 2) move the story forward? If not, consider cutting it.

15. Don't let your characters turn into little you's. The reader should not sense that you are lurking behind each page, pulling the strings of your puppets.

16. Bring out your characters' relevant flaws and foibles. Writing memoir is hard enough without your own personal scold going, "Tsk, tsk, Aunt Ellen isn't going to like *that!*" If you want people to read your memoir, you have to write stories about interesting people who seem real—that is, unpredictable. Realistic characters make mistakes, do distasteful things, sometimes even smell bad and pick their noses.

17. Make characters memorable by revealing a couple of salient features. At least four critical elements help create our impression of someone: gender, age, vocation, and manner. Manner is a person's personal bearing, one's habitual stance and style. When you show a middle-age woman as loud and pushy, you define her more sharply than you do by describing her blue eyes or big nose.

18. Bring characters to life by showing their emotions. Don't shy away from emotions, even if you've been macho your whole life. To show what matters to your characters, have them react to something that affects them. If, for example, your father lost his ranch to a bank, manned a picket line, or stood in line at a soup kitchen, actions that suggest emotional content, we want to know about it.

To show a character's emotion, visit that emotion in your own past. Were you ever so angry with someone you wanted to kill him? What was your behavior at that moment? Did you tremble, clench your jaw, punch a wall? Apply those reactions to your characters.

19. Provide background for your characters, though not necessarily at the beginning of the story. Background can be summed up as "reasons why"—reasons why a character does the things he does; reasons why he doesn't do other things.

You build a character's background to:

- Show the character's uniqueness.

- Show the character's reasons for behaving a certain way.

- Make the character believable and provide depth.

How much background is enough? Usually only enough to make your reader believe in the character, enough to make his emotional state clear and understandable. If your father, a main character in your story, is a raving, evangelical alcoholic, and you provide no explanation for his behavior, readers will feel frustrated—and they won't get to know your father.

Think of background in terms of four elements: body, environment, experience, and ideas.

Body. This is ancestry, heredity, genetic roots. It also includes the physical body, appearance. Why is this important? A skinny, uncoordinated adolescent has a different world view than a football star.

Environment. This is a character's milieu. Everyone is a product of his or her environment, both the geographical and social setting. When portraying a character, ask yourself, to what societies does this person give allegiance? A doctor, for example, can be both an American and a member of the American Medical Association. Maybe your character is a communist, a Republican, an Elk, an Iranian.

Experience. This is what shapes people, certainly, but it's not just our experiences that create misery or joy, but how we react to those experiences. Insult one man and he brushes it off; insult another and he starts swinging.

Ideas. Ideas shape you and the characters you write about. To the extent that you know these things, let your characters think, let them believe, let them explore unique alleyways of opinion. Give them private concepts to ponder. The grandfather who railed against FDR and the New Deal may have been a pain in the ass to live with, but he sounds like a good subject for a storyteller like you.

Example

Consider the following story told in two ways.

> *A man was taking a walking trip. Some thieves beat him up and left him. One passerby saw the hurt man and avoided him; and so did another traveler. But the third traveler was kind. He took care of the hurt man.*

Despite the conflict, it's a story bereft of human interest. The characters aren't shown doing anything; the writer is just telling us they're doing something. Compare this version:

> *A certain man went down from Jerusalem to Jericho, and fell among thieves, which stripped him of his raiment, and wounded him, and departed, leaving him half dead. and by chance there came down a certain priest that way; and when he saw him, he passed by on the other side. And likewise a Levite, when he was at the place, came and looked on him, and passed by on the other side. But a certain Samaritan, as he journeyed, came where he was; and when he saw him, he had compassion on him, and went to him, and bound up his wounds, pouring in oil and wine, and set him on his own beast, and brought him to an inn, and took care of him. and on the morrow when he departed, he took out two pence, and gave them to the host and said unto him, 'Take care of him; and whatsoever thou spendest more, when I come again, I will repay thee.'*

This is the original story of the Good Samaritan from the New Testament. We may not know what our hero looks like or how he's dressed, but from action after action, a picture of a good, charitable man emerges that has endured for two thousand years.

Exercise

Craft a short profile of someone you know, using some of the techniques above.

_____

_____

_____

_____

_____

_____

_____

_____

_____

_____

_____

Appendix M

Embrace Conflict

Example

Read the following plot outline for a story entitled "Runaway," and identify the types of conflict.

> Sue walks home from school with Eddie, her boyfriend. They stop a few blocks from her house. She is not supposed to be seeing Eddie because her parents disapprove of him. They say he is not good enough for her. Unknown to Sue and Eddie, her mother is driving by and sees her with Eddie.
>
> Sue arrives home. Her mother is waiting for her and they argue about Eddie. Sue believes that her parents don't understand her. Her mother counters that Sue is too young to understand what is good for her. Crying, Sue retreats to her room.
>
> Later that night, Sue decides to run away. She packs some things and slips out. She goes to Eddie's house. When she tells him what she's done, he tries to convince her that what she's doing won't solve the problem. She refuses to listen to him and dashes off before he can stop her.
>
> Eddie calls Sue's parents and tells them what happened. At first her parents don't believe him, but when Sue's mother checks

*her room, she realizes that Eddie is telling the truth. Together,
Eddie and Sue's parents begin searching for her.*

*It is late at night. Sue is waiting, alone, at a bus stop. She is
thinking about what Eddie said, how running away won't solve
the problem. She also thinks about her feelings for him and her
love for her parents. She slowly realizes that he is right. Finally,
she decides to go home.*

Exercises

Look for conflict in the stories you read and the movies you watch, and
note how it arises from the plot. Is the conflict man (kind) against man? Man
against environment? Man against society? Or man against himself? Which
makes the best story? Why?

Do a short, dialogue-driven piece that shows conflict between two or more
people.

Appendix N

Show, Don't Tell

Analyze the two passages below. Jot down at least three detailed reasons why the second version is better.

Tell: "My boss was a mean, heartless jerk. He yelled at me all the time, and exploited me in every way that he could. I was overworked, grossly underpaid, and never had a chance of going anywhere in my job."

Show: "I was just picking up my raincoat to leave when my boss's shout stopped me. 'Where do you think you're going?' he demanded. I turned around to see that his face was beet red and he was nearly pulling out his hair plugs in frustration. His wife had just called and they were having problems; I knew that much. And the Epstein case was driving him demented. We had less than four days to close, and no deal was in sight. I was exhausted, though, and I just wanted out of there. I had worked twelve-hour days for three weeks. How would I explain another late night of work to my husband, especially when the words 'overtime pay' weren't in my boss's vocabulary? I was grateful for the job and the chance to prove myself, but not enough to drive myself to an early grave."

Exercises

1. The following statements *tell*. Rewrite them, adding detail to create a picture, and make them *show*.

- Brett was scatterbrained.

  _____
  _____
  _____
  _____
  _____

- Hailee was sad.

  _____
  _____
  _____
  _____
  _____

- Sydney was in love.

  _____
  _____
  _____
  _____
  _____

- Des was a hot-headed basketball coach.

  _____
  _____
  _____
  _____
  _____

2. Replace each of the following adjective-noun combinations (which tend to tell) with a more powerful noun-verb combination (which tends to show). For example, nervous actor might become actor fidgeted.

- Embarrassed girl

  _____
  _____
  _____
  _____

- Impatient trucker

_____
_____
_____
_____

- Angry politician

_____
_____
_____
_____

- Despondent widower

_____
_____
_____
_____

- Overheated engine

_____
_____
_____
_____

- Nervous elephant

_____
_____
_____
_____

The storyteller's responsibility is not to be wise; the storyteller is the person who creates an atmosphere in which wisdom can reveal itself.

–Barry Lopez

Appendix O

Favor the Active Voice

Exceptions

Use of the passive voice is sometimes appropriate.

1. Use the passive voice when the actor is not known.

Peter Jansen was attacked and badly beaten while walking through the park last night.

Since the writer presumably does not know who attacked Peter, she is forced to use the passive voice, or to resort to an even clumsier alternative such as: "Some person or persons unknown attacked and badly beat Peter Jansen while he walked in the park last night."

The play was first performed in 1591.

The sentence suggests that though there is a record of the performance, there may be no record of the performers. Or maybe who did the performing is not important to the writer.

2. Use the passive voice when the result or the receiver of the action is more important than the actor.

The experiment was finished on June 16. On June 17 the results were reviewed by the advisory board and reported immediately to the Pentagon.

The new bridge was completed in April.

In these sentences, we have little interest in who completed the bridge, performed the experiments, or reported the results. The important things are the bridge, the experiment, the review, and the report.

3. Use the passive voice for emphasis or surprise when there is a punch line.

The gold medal in the bobsled competition was won by a six-year-old boy!

Exercises

1. Write three sentences in which the passive voice is justified.

_____

_____

_____

_____

_____

_____

_____

_____

_____

_____

_____

2. Rewrite the following sentences to eliminate the passive voice—and thus the wordiness.

   a. *For three years, the company newsletter was written and edited by me.*

   _____

   _____

   _____

   b. *The staff was instructed by Mr. Pierce in the use of the new lathe.*

   _____

   _____

   _____

   c. *A guide to the most recent tax exemptions was put together by Fred.*

   _____

   _____

   _____

   d. *Karen was hired by Louis to shine his shoes.*

   _____

   _____

   _____

   e. *A feasibility study was conducted by Nancy.*

   _____

   _____

   _____

Appendix P

Find the Humor

Example

Although few events are more detestable than the dentist appointment, Bill Bryson, in his memoir *The Life and Times of the Thunderbolt Kid*, manages to keep us from turning away by presenting its lighter side.

> *The slowest place of all in my corner of the youthful firmament was the large cracked-leather dental chair of Dr. D.K. Brewster, our spooky, cadaverous dentist, while waiting for him to assemble his instruments and get down to business. There time didn't move at all. It just hung.*

> *Dr. Brewster was the most unnerving dentist in America. He was, for one thing, about 108 years old and had more than a touch of Parkinsonism in his wobbly hands. Nothing about him inspired confidence. He was perennially surprised by the power of his own equipment. "Whoa!" he'd say as he briefly enlivened some screaming device or other. "You could do some damage with that, I bet."*

> *Worse still, he didn't believe in novocaine. He thought it dangerous and unproven. When Dr. Brewster, humming mindlessly, drilled through rocky molar and found the pulpy mass of tender nerve within, it could make your toes burst out the front of your shoes.*

We appeared to be his only patients. I used to wonder why our father put us through this seasonal nightmare, and then I heard Dr. Brewster congratulating him one day for his courageous frugality and I understood at once, for my father was the twentieth century's cheapest man. "There is no point in putting yourself to the danger and expense of novocaine for anything less than the whole or partial removal of a jaw," Dr. Brewster was saying.

"Absolutely," my father agreed. Actually he said something more like "Abmmfffmmfff," as he had just stepped from Dr. Brewster's chair and wouldn't be able to speak intelligibly for at least three days, but he nodded with feeling.

"I wish more people felt like you, Mr. Bryson," Dr. Brewster added. "That will be three dollars, please."

Appendix Q

Revise Your Work

Some authors weigh in on the art and necessity of revision:

I believe more in the scissors than I do in the pencil. –Truman Capote

Sit down, and put down everything that comes into your head and then you're a writer. But an author is one who can judge his own stuff's worth, without pity, and destroy most of it –Colette

Good things, when short, are twice as good. –Gracián

If a teacher told me to revise, I thought that meant my writing was a broken-down car that needed to go to the repair shop. I felt insulted. I didn't realize the teacher was saying, "Make it shine. It's worth it." Now I see revision as a beautiful word of hope. It's a new vision of something. It means you don't have to be perfect the first time. What a relief! –Naomi Shihab Nye

I can't write five words but that I change seven. –Dorothy Parker

You write to communicate to the hearts and minds of others what's burning inside you and we edit to let the fire show through the smoke. –Arthur Polotnik

Editing should be, especially in the case of old writers, a counseling rather than a collaborating task. The tendency of the writer-editor to collaborate is natural, but he should say to himself, "How can I help this writer to say it better in his

own style?" and avoid "How can I show him how I would write it, if it were my piece?" –James Thurber

I notice that you use plain, simple language, short words and brief sentences. That is the way to write English—it is the modern way and the best way. Stick to it; don't let fluff and flowers and verbosity creep in. When you catch an adjective, kill it. No, I don't mean utterly, but kill most of them, then the rest will be valuable. They weaken when they are close together. They give strength when they are wide apart. An adjective habit, or a wordy, diffuse, flowery habit, once fastened upon a person, is as hard to get rid of as any other vice. –Mark Twain

A kiss that speaks volumes is seldom a first edition. –Clare Whiting

Writing is not like painting, where you add. It is not what you put on the canvas that the reader sees. Writing is more like a sculpture where you remove, you eliminate, in order to make the work visible. Even those pages you remove somehow remain. –Elie Wiesel

Exercise

The following writing sample, taken from a website, is rife with mistakes. Look closely and you will find an impressive array of punctuation, grammar, spelling, syntax, and typographical errors. Edit to make it readable.

EVEREST INTRODUCTION

Hi there I have started a homepage that will tell you everything you ever wanted to know about the Mountain. Well I hope you will read on and remind I you that parts are still under construction.

I just finished reading "Into Thin Air" by Jon Krakauer and reccomend you read it if your interested in learning more about how expeditions work. He Talks about what happened on the 1996 Everest Expeditions. He also gives a brief history of Everest. If you enjoyed reading into thin Air you might also be interested in reading "Into The Wild" and "Eiger Dreams" which he also wrote. Ive read both of those and highly reccomend them. I resently just finished reading a book called The Climb that was written by Anatoli Boukreev. He was the lead guide on Scott Fischers team and this book is writing about his experiances. I enjoyed the book and recommend reading it to anyone who wants to learn more about what happend on the 1996 tragedy. What have people thought of the book? What kind of impressions did you get from the book?"

Mt Everest is located in Northeastern Nepal and stands 29028 feet above sea level. Everest was first attempted in 1921 by a group led by George Mallory but it was not intill 1953 when New Zealander Sir Edmand Hillary and Sherpa Tenzing Norgay made the summit via the south col route. It was not untill 1963 that the first American expedition made it when Seattle native Jim Whittaker summited with Sherpa Nawang Gombu. A pair of other climbers on that expedition also where the first climbers to climb the West ridge. To date some 4000 people have tried to climb Everest, around 660 have succeeded and 142 have died (based on 1996 features).

Appendix R

Choose Good Topics

Here is a partial list of memoir topics. It is meant to trigger general memories only. Once you've selected a topic—say, family pets—then zero in on a specific pet in a specific incident—such as the time Snuffy helped you solve a bank robbery. Start with topics that lend themselves to emotional content.

1. Your Earliest Recollection

2. Your First Home

3. Childhood Years

4. Toys of Childhood

5. Family Pets

6. Seasons and What They Meant to You as a Child

7. A Favorite Snapshot

8. Parents

9. Grandparents

10. Sisters and Brothers

11. Early School Years

12. Junior High Years: Adolescence

13. High School Years: Future Dreams

14. A Family Gathering Place

15. Early Vacations

16. Military Years

17. The Great Depression

18. World War II

19. Work Life

20. Courtship/Wedding

21. Spouse

22. Early Married Years

23. Birth and Life of First Child

24. Raising a Family

25. Neighbors

26. A Dear Friend

27. Family Customs/Habits

28. A Chosen Relative

29. When the Children Leave Home

30. Weddings

31. In-Laws

32. Grandchildren

33. Life as a Widow/Widower

34. Retirement Years

35. When I Look Back, I Wish I Had . . .

36. As I Look Ahead, I Plan To . . .

37. A Happy Period in Your Life

38. A Difficult Period

39. A Major Change/Turning Point

40. A Memorable Event in Your Life

41. A Narrow Escape

42. Your Worst Mistake

43. A Smart Decision

44. A Special Accomplishment

45. Involvement in the Community

46. Unusual Trip/Adventure/ Vacation

47. Hobbies and Leisure Interests

48. Family Recipes

49. Artifacts/Keepsakes/ Heirlooms

50. Values and Ideals From Your Parents

51. Religion, Philosophy, Faith Over the Years

52. A Catastrophic Event/ Experience

53. Your Favorite Holiday

54. A Memorable Christmas

55. A Special Family Event

56. A Person Who Influenced Your Life

57. A Life or Lives You Have Touched

58. Favorite Places

59. Transportation Over the Years

60. Political Interests

61. Fashions Over the Years

62. Entertainment

63. Health and Illness

64. Searching for Roots

65. Risks Encountered

66. Losses in Your Life

67. Biggest Surprise

68. Most Embarrassing Moment

69. Most Frightening Moment

70. Travel

71. Death

Appendix S

The Art of Critique

Regardless of your skills or goals, you should welcome critical input. If possible, get a second, third, and fourth opinion. Whether you read to a group or show your work to another person, learn the art of giving and receiving criticism.

Giving Criticism

1. Be honest and objective in your criticism. You seldom do the author a favor when you hold back on a critique. No need to be harsh, but you should identify any significant problems with the work.

2. Be as specific as possible in your critique. Take note of the following elements of the story: plot, structure, setting, characterization, point of view, pacing, transitions, dialogue, conflict, sensory detail. It's frustrating to receive a vague, rambling critique. Point out specific aspects of the piece that worked or didn't work for you, and tell why. Example: "I don't believe the Jeffrey character is less useful to the author" than "I don't buy the Jeffrey character because his motivation for giving up his military career was unclear.

3. Be concise with a classroom critique. Remember that time is limited in a meeting, so don't belabor a point. Say what you have to say and let the next person have a say.

4. Don't repeat another classmate's critique. If someone gives the same criticism you were going to offer, simply say, "I agree," and move on, unless you can substantially expand on another's critique.

5. Criticize the manuscript, not the author. Trying to second-guess the author's intent or motivation is not your job. Just state what worked or didn't work for you in the story, and why.

6. Make statements—don't ask questions. Asking the author questions invites time-consuming debate. Instead of asking, "Why did Anna throw out the teakettle?" say "It's not clear to me why Anna threw out the teakettle" or "I don't understand why Anna threw out the teakettle."

7. Identify your biases. It's important to let an author know if he's hit one of your hot buttons. If, for example, the author writes a story about a woman who has an abortion, which you oppose, the objectivity of your critique may be colored by your personal beliefs. Do the author a favor by disclosing that.

8. Balance your critique as much as possible. An unbroken series of negative comments, though perhaps honest, can be painful. Compliment whenever possible. Be tactful and end on a positive note.

Receiving Criticism

When your work is being critiqued, you should:

- Take notes. Even if you disagree with a criticism, take note of it. Later you may see it differently.

- Be an attentive listener. Your improvement as a writer depends on your listening ability, not your speaking ability.

- Avoid defending yourself. Resist the temptation to interrupt with an explanation or clarification. Remember, you won't be able to explain or clarify with an editor, so just listen and take note that someone had a problem with that section. Address the problem later.

Appendix T

Freewrite Through Writer's Block

Many writers have unclogged the pipes with a freewrite, which is merely writing uninhibitedly for 5, 10, or 15 minutes at a time. If you get stuck, write the same word over and over until you unstick. Or counter with a dash and write, "What I really want to say is . . ." and go on writing. You're more interested in process than product.

Keep your hand moving and let your imagination soar. Fantasize. Follow your hunches and intuition. Stretch your mind. Lose control and don't worry about punctuation or grammar. Find your wild mind. But be specific (not car, Cadillac; not fruit, apple).

Author Kate Green once said, "If you want to write, you have to be willing to be disturbed." Write about what disturbs you, what you fear, what you have not been able to speak about.

Suggested Openers

I remember . . .
I'm thinking of . . .
I want to write about . . .
I know . . .
I am . . .
I want . . .
I don't want . . .
I love . . .
I hate . . .

Exercises

1. Find a sentence that comes from somewhere deep within. For example: "I fell in love with my life one scorching summer afternoon . . ."

2. Write about doing something you really loved, a time when you felt whole and complete in an activity for its own sake, a time when you concentrated fully on something.

3. List things that please you and then write about one of them, something you chose all for yourself, not because your parents liked it.

4. Go back to childhood, give yourself a magical power you once wished for, and write from that place.

Appendix U

The Art of the Interview

Here are some tips for interviewing experts, whether it's Dad or Donald Trump.

Before the Interview

- Research the subject's background and views. Don't alienate your subject by showing basic ignorance of his work and life. If basic demographic questions, such as age and schooling, can be answered elsewhere, you save time and make the interview more interesting for your expert.

- Plan your questions, especially at first, but don't read them too formally or artificially.

- Decide how you'll record the interview. Like most writers, I use a tape recorder. A tape recorder is actually less intrusive than notetaking, as it's soon forgotten. It also leaves you free to listen and to jot down notes for future questions.

- Prepare everything you want to take to the interview, including pads, pens, pencils, recorder with new batteries, extra batteries, blank tapes, supplementary background or research materials, and a camera if you plan to take pictures. Just before you leave for the interview, double-check that 1) you have everything, and 2) it's all working.

- When you contact the subject, convey in words and tone that you are a good person, that this is a worthy project, and that the subject is key to the story.

- Arrange to meet someplace quiet. A restaurant or coffee shop may work if it's not too busy. Outside, beware of urban noise.

- If the interview is brief or meeting your subject is too difficult, consider conducting a telephone interview. The simplest way: Put the subject on a speaker phone and record it or take notes. If you record, always ask permission first.

During the Interview

- Dress appropriately for the subject. If you're talking to the CEO of General Motors in his office, you will dress differently than if meeting a lumberjack in the forest.

- Let your subjects talk. Allow digressions to a point. Sometimes good material emerges from digressions, but eventually you may have to guide them back with a pointed question.

- Create an informal conversational atmosphere that encourages your experts to loosen up. Get comfortable and ask them to do the same. Rearrange the seating if necessary. Have drinking water available.

- Check the acoustics. If necessary, close the door, turn off fans or radio, or move.

- Set up the tape recorder and mike. Align the mike so that you both can be heard without changing positions.

- Conduct a five-second monologue to check the recorder. Make adjustments as necessary.

- Ask if your subject has any preliminary questions or concerns.

- Agree on approximately how long the interview will last.

- Bring to bear all your powers of observation. Note not only what the subject says but how she says it, including tone and mannerisms.

- Ask for clarification, explanation, or elaboration, as needed.

- Before concluding, make sure you've asked all your questions, including whether the subject has any comments or questions. Be gracious to the end. Ask for permission to re-contact with follow-up questions, if need be. Get appropriate email addresses and phone numbers. Consider sending a thank-you note or email.

Example

Studs Terkel was the master interviewer. He crisscrossed the country interviewing American workers, which he included in his bestselling books, such as *Hard Times*, *The Good War*, and *Working*. During his countless interviews, he put his subjects at ease and lured from them confessions, dreams, fears—their stories.

Terkel, who died in 2008, wanted this as his epitaph: "Curiosity did not kill this cat."

Exercises

1. Interview two senior citizens about how things have changed in their lifetime. Some possible questions:

   - Where did you live growing up? Which place did you like the best? Why?

   - What person or persons had the greatest influence on your life? Why?

   - When do you remember paying for things? What did things cost? A loaf of bread? A quart of milk? Is it easier or harder to make ends meet today?

   - What historical events do you remember? For example: The 1929 Stock Market Crash; the Hindenburg disaster of 1937; the bombing of Pearl Harbor; the assassination of President Kennedy. Such events might be called "generational benchmarks." Although people seem to recall disasters first, try to elicit memories of cultural events, too. Older folks might remember when Joe Louis knocked out German heavyweight champion Max Schmeling in 1938. Younger ones might remember when boxer/poet Muhammad Ali refused to go fight in Vietnam.

   - How did you find the person you married? What drew you together? If divorced, what tore you apart?

- Did you have children? How did they change your life?

- Can you recall expressions that you used as a young person? For example: "bee's knees"; "cat's pajamas"; "swell."

- What's the best thing about the world today compared to when you were young? The worst thing? In general, do you think things in the world are getting better or worse?

- If you could tell people today something and hope they would remember it, what would you tell them?

2. What would the two people you interviewed disagree about? Write a short dialogue between them to show that difference of opinion.

3. Ask some senior citizens what they would do differently if they had their life to live over. Here's how Nadine Stair, age 85, answered it in her now famous poem.

I'd Pick More Daisies

If I had my life to live over,
I'd try to make more mistakes next time.
I would relax. I would limber up.
I would be sillier than I have on this trip.

I would be crazier. I would be less hygienic.
I would take more chances, I would take more trips.
I would climb more mountains, swim more rivers, and watch more sunsets.
I would burn more gasoline. I would eat more ice cream and less beans.
I would have more actual troubles and fewer imaginary ones . . .

If I had to do it over again, I would go places and do things. I'd travel lighter
than I have.
If I had my life to live over, I would start barefooted earlier in the spring and
stay that way later in the fall.
I would play hooky more. I wouldn't make such good grades except by
accident.
I would ride on merry-go-rounds.

I'd pick more daisies!

Appendix V

Master the Query Letter

Author Earma Brown points to seven major mistakes that query writers make:

Mistake #1. Failure to Value One's Expertise

All writers have life experiences to draw from. Yet many undervalue them, focusing only on writing experience. If, for example, you have an idea of training tips for toddlers, mention that you raised three toddlers.

Mistake #2. Failure to Develop Ideas Fully

Your query letter is a sales pitch that must convince the editor you have more than just a one-sentence idea. Do the research necessary to support your ideas.

Mistake #3. Failure to Think Creatively

Either the story or the presentation must be fresh.

Mistake #4. Failure to Read Publication

Familiarize yourself with the style and tone of the publication you wish to query. Look at the latest issues to see how your piece might fit the editor's needs.

Mistake #5. Failure to Follow Professional Query Etiquette

Address your query to a specific editor. Check the masthead or Writer's Market for the correct editor's name.

Mistake #6. Failure to Accept Free Assignments

A good way to jumpstart your writing credits is to accept unpaid assignments, especially if you receive a byline.

Mistake #7. Failure to Respect Editor

Most editors won't blacklist you if you follow up with one email, but annoying them with a stream of emails or calls shows a lack of respect for their time.

Examples

One option is to lead your query with an excerpt from the work itself, as below. What do you think of the following query leads? Do they make you want to read on? Why or why not?

> *After putting it off for three years, Larry Cassoll limped into a podiatrist's office with a 22-caliber bullet still lodged in his foot . . .*

> *Six teenagers sit cross-legged on the floor facing a young man who has been invited to speak to them. The room is warm and comfortable, more of a living room than a classroom. The door is closed and a "Do Not Disturb" sign hangs on the other side. The lighting is subdued so that no one will see a blush or a tremble. "I'm a faggot," the young man says. "I'm a fruit, a pansy, a gay." He pauses. "I'm a homosexual," he says. "and I'm a human being just like you."*

Appendix W

Collaborate with an Agent

Here are some dos and don'ts when soliciting a literary agent to represent your work to publishers.

Do

- Familiarize yourself with the agent's submission guidelines, usually found on their websites.

- Research agents' backgrounds on Websites and message boards, such as AgentResearch.com's agent-verification service, AbsoluteWrite.com's "Bewares and Background Check" forum, and Anotherrealm.com's "Predators and Editors" page.

- Make sure the agent you query deals in the genre you're pitching. Don't send a young-adult novel to an agent who doesn't accept that type of fiction.

- Query the agent first rather than sending the manuscript.

- Make the query letter clean and professional. Address it to a specific person (rather than "to whom it may concern") and spell her name right. In fact, spell everything right and exorcise all typos.

- Include a self-addressed stamped envelope (SASE) with your submission.

Don't

- Query by email unless the agent's submission guidelines give you permission.

- Expect an agent to edit your work—if your manuscript needs editing, get it done beforehand.

- Accept an agent who charges upfront fees. Agents should make money by selling authors' works, not by charging reading fees.

- Harass the agent with phone calls or letters. Some agents respond to queries immediately; others take months. Once an agent's specified response time has run out, then it's okay to follow up. In the meantime, work on your next project.

Important Information

Agent listings will contain a wealth of facts. Pay special attention to the following:

1. AAR membership: Many agents are members of AAR, the Association of Authors' Representatives, which means they subscribe to a specific code of ethics, such as not charging upfront fees.

2. Stats: What percentage of clients are new, unpublished writers?

3. Needs: Is the agent looking for fiction or nonfiction or both?

4. What the agent doesn't want.

5. How to contact.

6. How long the agent takes to respond.

7. Whether the agent accepts simultaneous submissions.

8. Recent sales.

Appendix X

Consider Self-Publishing

Self-Publishing Tips

- Don't skimp on quality. Self-publishing is not vain or an admission that your work is not good enough for a mainstream publisher. But if your self-published work is not the best you can do, then the effort is vain, and unfair to your readers and yourself. Make sure the final product is attractive and clean. Spend the time checking every detail, exorcizing every error. Consider having a copy editor do the final edit.

- If you have a highly specialized audience, self-publishing may be ideal. Commercial publishers are often unwilling to go after such an audience. But self-publishers can target them with specific promotions, publicity, and marketing efforts. The first time I took a publishing class, I sat next to a young man who had self-published a book on marijuana cultivation and sold 100,000 copies.

- Before you publish your book, assess the market. Determine whether there is a need for your book. Develop a picture in your mind of who is likely to want, need, use, or buy it. The existence of other books on the same subject does not automatically preclude another. Look how many biographies of Elvis and Marilyn have been published.

- Plan to spend time promoting your work. One easy, inexpensive way to spread the word is to do radio interviews. You can usually do the interview from home.

- Shop around for the right printing company. Printers differ enormously in what they can do and what they charge. Even with shipping costs, it may be cheaper to have your book published abroad.

- Send free copies to reviewing agencies. Before publication, consider sending the manuscript to prominent people to get their endorsements.

- Get your book into bookstores and other venues that sell books. You can contact local bookstores, which will almost always take your book. But typically they will buy only two or three, and the burden falls on you to monitor sales and make sure they reorder. A better option is to hook up with a distributor for small presses.

- Consider mail-order sales to individuals, libraries, and other organizations.

- Make sure your book has an ISBN number, is properly copyrighted, and is listed in *Forthcoming Books* and *Books in Print*.

- Don't neglect the business aspects of the operation. Promotion and sales will cut into your writing time, but that effort is critical for success.

- If your self-published book sells well, you can approach major publishers with it, either on your own or through an agent. Successful self-published books have gone on to achieve second and even third printings with major presses.

- Consult one of the many books on the subject for more information about self-publishing, and read on . . .

Self-Publishing Step by Step

Step 1: Write and Design Your Manuscript

- First, make sure your subject is interesting to you. Do you like it well enough to spend hours and hours on it? Years ago I began to write a long piece on flea markets. I was twenty hours into the project before I realized . . . I don't like flea markets.

- Create a detailed Table of Contents. This tells you where you're going with your story.

- Keep your material organized and easily accessible. For every category and subcategory, create a labeled file folder.

- Write your back-cover sales copy early. The back-cover text will tell you exactly what the book is about and who will be interested. Stating that clearly in the beginning will keep you on track. As a guide, read the back-cover copy of other books.

- Shop around for editors, proofreaders, cover artists, and book designers to help you. Check ads in *Writer's Digest* and other publications; consult a local writer's group. Find people whose writing styles, personalities, and interests match yours.

- Find a proofreader to review your final draft. This person should be an excellent grammarian who has not seen your work. Such "cold readers" will catch errors that others miss. Make the manuscript as perfect as you can before you go to print.

- Once you finish the manuscript, acquire necessary permissions. Fair use in the industry is considered to be 250-300 words, so if you've quoted more than that, get the publisher's permission or paraphrase to reduce the quote. If you paraphrase, say so.

- Get testimonials. Bind a few advance copies for review by authorities in your field. Consider asking an expert to write a back-cover endorsement or a foreword (you can offer to write it and submit it to the expert for his or her approval).

- Set your book's price. To calculate the price, figure all your costs, including design and layout, printing, mailing, and at least $1 per book for promotion. Price the tax and shipping fees separately. Remember, you will seldom receive full cover price for the books you sell. Bookstores, for example, typically receive at least a 40 percent discount.

- Order your bar code.

- Spend time on your book cover. Most of your design budget should be devoted to the cover, your key selling tool. Unless you have talent in this area, hire a cover designer.

- Choose the book's size and binding. Decide whether you want paperback or hardcover. Learn about the different types of binding.

- Choose paper, art, and photos. These are all part of your book's visual appeal. Critique other books for art, graphics, and paper quality. If money is tight, consider uncopyrighted clip art.

Step 2: Choose Your Printer

- Don't let geography limit your choices. Reputable printers exist throughout the world, and technology makes it easy to deal with companies thousands of miles away. You can find printers by searching book-printing directories or by working with a print broker. Choose a specialist in book printing that promises the best quality for the best price.

- Send a "Request for Quotation" (RFQ) to at least a dozen printers. Set a deadline for all printers to respond. Ask each for brochures, planning kits, paper samples, and a copy of one of their printed books. Before selecting a printer, compare price quotes, turnaround time, and the quality of the sample books.

- Check out the printer's reputation for fiscal responsibility. You don't want your book tied up in a bankruptcy proceeding.

- Control your print run. Print only the number of books you expect to sell in the first year. This will cost more per book than a larger print run, but you don't want to end up with a roomful of books that you can't sell.

- Retain the rights to your material. By insisting on ownership of all plates and disks, you can reprint with a different company, if you wish. Consult a literary lawyer about this matter.

- Send camera-ready materials to the printer with written instructions. Put everything in writing, including who is responsible for any changes made during the printing process.

- Scrutinize the bluelines. Bluelines, or printer's proofs, are your final chance to correct errors. Review bluelines with your editor and proofreader. After this phase, any mistakes will be repeated in every copy of your book, so make the effort to eliminate them.

- Stay in touch with your printer. At each stage of the book-production process, ask questions and make sure you understand the answers.

- Relish the moment when the books arrive on your doorstep. This is what the effort has been for—seeing your work in print. Enjoy it, however briefly, for tomorrow you go to work promoting and distributing the damn thing.

Step 3: Promote Your Book

- Send out review copies. Put a copy of your book in the hands of anyone who can help you. When I published *RISK!*, I sent free copies to *Backpacker* and *Outside* magazines, and any others I thought might review it. Collect favorable reviews to use as testimonials.

- Consider developing a press kit. To other media outlets that might be interested in you or your book, send a press release, a photo of yourself, and a photo of your book's cover.

- Consider doing a mailing. Targeted mailing lists are available for a nominal fee. But the mailing itself will cost, and most direct mailings elicit less than a 1 percent response. Do the math.

- Do book signings. Take your book into bookstores and discuss with the owner the feasibility of scheduling a book signing.

- Offer your book as a premium gift. Sometimes businesses, such as insurance companies and banks, buy books and give them to their patrons as promotional gifts.

- Send your book to the Book-of-the-Month Club and the like. It may not be a big money maker, but can boost your status and reputation.

- Tap into the Internet. The Internet offers global, often free, publicity. Place your book with online booksellers, such as Amazon.com, or consider promoting it on your own website.

- Get listed in trade publications, such as *Books in Print, Publishers' Trade List Annual*, and *Publishers Weekly*.

- Do talk shows. As an author, you are considered an expert on your book's subject, and thus a candidate for talk shows, especially radio.

- Make personal appearances. Make speaking dates at conventions, conferences, workshops, and seminars, and sell your book before, during, and after your appearance.

- Be innovative. Seek out nontraditional bookstores. Barter for books or services. Come up with new ideas.

- Be prepared. Carry books, brochures, and business cards wherever you go.

Step 4: Distribute Your Book

- Ship the first books. Send the first two copies to the United States Copyright Office and one copy to the Library of Congress. Mail copies to the people who bought your book before publication.

- Find wholesalers and distributors. Read the yellow pages and visit bookstores to learn the preferred wholesalers and distributors. Set up appointments with their representatives. Be prepared to negotiate your cut of the book's cover price.

- Market to libraries. Libraries usually purchase at full cover price and rarely return books. Consult *Bates Directory of US Public Libraries*.

- Approach catalog companies. Pitch your book to catalog companies that sell goods related to your subject. They typically place large orders, don't return books, and expect large discounts.

- Explore foreign markets. Place a free listing in *Cumulative Book Index*, subscribed to by libraries and booksellers throughout the world.

- Pitch your book to schools. After I published *RISK!*, I sent a mailing to California junior colleges and sold several class sets.

- Exhibit at book trade shows and conventions, where you can showcase your book to thousands of booksellers, distributors, and corporate buyers.

- Consider selling to government agencies and private associations. If you have the right subject, these can be large, lucrative markets.

SOME MEMOIRS

Double, Double, Caldron Bubble

Sylvia B. Bailin

One evening I bypassed dinner to rush to an early performance of *Macbeth*. By Act IV, the Three Witches stirring that steaming caldron reminded me I'd eaten no more than an apple for lunch. They simmered "eye of newt and toe of frog," but my brain signaled "pot of soup."

My hunger grew along with the Macbeths' appetite for power. By the end of the banquet scene, I was ready to nosh!

With the tingling in my belly, my desires turned to deli.

On my way home, my late-night Safeway lured me, and I veered into the parking lot—on the bakery side. Pot of soup no longer applied. The automated doors hissed open, the Witches' hell-gates.

Double, double, toil and trouble,

Fire burn and caldron bubble.

As I arrived in the bakery department, the will that fights irrational impulse vanished as by a wizard's wand. In its place was joy at the prospect that lay ahead. I lingered over the baked goods, increasing my pleasure with mouth-watering delay.

Whipped meringue pies, chocolate cakes,

Drizzled strudels, blissful makes.

In my state of sweet surrender, I grappled with choice. Croissants? Too airy. Sugar doughnuts? Too greasy. Chocolate chip cookies? No class.

Then I saw it, under its tight, clear plastic wrap. A darling, five-inch delicately browned pie, so flaky that tiny crumbs lay about its fluted rim. Out of the crust's dainty dime-size window oozed crushed strawberry filling, calling me. I answered, "Yes."

In my kitchen, with ceremony and delicious anticipation, I disrobed my sweetie-pie, cut it in half (some for tomorrow), and placed a half on an elegant gold-trimmed plate. I set out a cloth napkin and fork, then seated myself before my feast.

Slowly, I cut into the pie with the side of my fork. Juices oozed forth. That first piece flooded my senses: the berry fragrance on its way to my mouth, the soft crust yielding to lemony sharpness, the subtle scrunch of tiny seeds. Almost too exquisite to swallow.

But I did, again and again. Soon I had consumed the other half, too, my pledge for tomorrow lost in passion's appetite. Like Macbeth's murders, the second killing was easier.

Late that night, I paid penance. Bilious indigestion. Heartburn. I stared into the dark, feeling betrayed by that not-so-darling pie. Its image rose up, like Banquo's ghost. With each intestinal rumble I saw visions of berries, red as Macbeth's blood.

Seeds of berry, crust of lard,

Cramps intestines doubly hard.

Double, double, toil and trouble,

Fire burn and caldron bubble

With the dawn, my home remedies took effect and I lay in bed, exhausted. A caution returned, old but renewed by the thrust of fresh experience: Remember the tyranny of passionate appetite—tomorrow and tomorrow and tomorrow.

Trailhead

Steve Boga

1958: We have been studying this weird guy John Muir in school. He used to hike around in the high mountains with only a blanket and a few biscuits, and today I got to see the trail that's named after him. Mom, Dad, and I are camping in Yosemite Valley, where Muir hung out a lot. This morning, Dad took me to Happy Isles, to the start (they call it the "trailhead") of the John Muir Trail. We stood there for what seemed like a long time, just staring at the trail sign, a big old iron thing with stenciled names and numbers that looked like it might have been around when Muir himself first stood there. It listed nice-sounding places like Sunrise and Palisade lakes, and incredible distances! "Mount Whitney: 212 miles" I can't imagine walking that far.

A couple of hikers wearing green backpacks and carrying fishing gear walked up from the parking lot. They stopped for a second to read the sign, then gave each other kind of strained smiles and headed up the trail with real determination. I watched them a long time. I couldn't help wondering: "Where are they going? How long will they will be gone?"

When I looked at my father's face, I could tell he was thinking the same thing. Then he took my hand—which he never does—and led me to the other side of the sign. "There, you're on the John Muir Trail," he said. "We're at the lowest point—4,034 feet above sea level."

A few minutes later, while we were sitting on a rock eating some dried fruit and stale sandwiches, listening to the friendly roar of the Merced River, Dad said, "You know, I've always wanted to hike the John Muir Trail, all 212 miles of it." It wasn't so much what he said but how he said it that got to me. He sounded full of regret, like he'd missed out on something really important. It made me feel kind of sad. And eating the stale sandwich he'd made, well, that just made me feel sadder. "I don't suppose I'll ever do it now. You have to put in food caches along the way. And you need a buddy to hike with."

For a second, I thought I might cry. At that moment, I figured I probably liked him better than I ever had. I looked up at him and smiled, and he smiled back, and I could tell he was wondering if I could ever be that buddy. He looked so darn hopeful that I wanted to hug him and tell him, "Oh, sure you will, Dad. Someday we'll do it as a team."

But we just aren't that way together.

1960: Today we all hiked the first couple of miles of the John Muir Trail, to the top of Vernal Falls. Mom said it was the most beautiful hike she'd ever taken. The guidebook she keeps in her knapsack calls it "a steep climb through a mist-enshrouded, granite-walled amphitheater." That sounds about right to me.

It was a steep climb all right, but I was so excited that I kept hiking ahead, pretending I was John Muir. Then I'd run back down and hike with Mom and Dad for a while, before blasting ahead to see how many more tourists I could pass (final count 234). Mom hikes slowly but does okay for her age, which is right up there. Dad goes slowly to stay with her and to take pictures.

At the top, we sat on a rock and had lunch. The sun was reflecting brightly off the white-grey granite, so I put on my dark glasses, feeling really cool. It was hot enough for me to take off my shirt. The sun seemed awfully strong, like it was digging little craters into my back. I've noticed a change in my senses since we got to the mountains. For one thing, the sky looks a lot bluer than ever before; for another, the pine and spruce trees smell sweeter; and the sounds—the buzzing insects, the squawking birds and squirrels, the wind moving through the leaves—seem sweeter, too. My mother says I might be getting a jump on puberty.

When we wanted to talk, we had to shout above the roar of Vernal Falls, which sounded like thunder that wouldn't quit. Dad spent most of our time looking up the trail toward Nevada Falls, Muir Pass, Mount Whitney—wondering what it was like up there, what adventures awaited anyone going all the way to Whitney.

It's like Dad and I share a secret now.

1962: Dad and I are halfway through a two-week backpacking trip in Yosemite, a lot of it on the John Muir Trail. Our packs are way too heavy (Dad brought a hatchet and a heavy camera, and together we brought enough food to make John Muir throw up.) And after a week alone, relations between us are sometimes about as chilly as the lakes we camp by.

Still, it has been an unforgettable trip and great in many ways. I have learned about boots, blisters, black bears, deer, mosquitoes, sleeping bags, pitching tents, building campfires, fishing, altitude, storms, glaciers, rock formations, crossing streams, untangling fishing line, white water, and the Belding ground squirrel. Though Dad has never concerned himself with my urban survival skills, he takes an active interest in my wilderness education.

I have decided I like the hiking best, the mosquitoes least. Hiking trails with a pack on my back makes me feel powerful and self-sufficient. And it's something I feel I'm good at. I wonder if I can get a job walking when I grow up.

1988: A funny thing happened for a while today—I did nothing. I was sitting on a patch of spongy meadow at the edge of Magic Lake (our name) on a windless seventy-five-degree day, my back against a tree, at peace with the world. Jeff was off somewhere and it was mountain quiet, a deep resounding silence broken only by the lapping of water against rocks and the happy hum of insects.

Suddenly it hit me that I'd been inert for maybe an hour. I hadn't read a book, written in my diary, or tried to catch a fish. My daypack, rod, and reel lay beside me, untouched.

In the city, where we all toil feverishly on treadmills of our own making, such contented repose is as rare as Belding ground squirrels. Alone, ten thousand feet above sea level, it seems as natural as the environment. If I were a therapist, I would prescribe high-altitude camping for my wigged-out patients.

1994: As I enter my "middle years," kicking and screaming, I still have not hiked the length of the John Muir Trail. So what? I have my whole life to do it, and what better goal to cling to? Actually, I have what seems an attainable goal: Three friends and I made a pact to hike the entire route in three installments. Next summer, we will do the first installment, 70 miles on a ten-day trip.

Splitting the trek into three segments, carrying fancy tents—it's a bit cushier than the hike my father envisioned. But who is he to say? Today he does most of his walking on the golf course and it's not his dream anymore. It's mine. He gave it to me and I plan to keep it as long as I can.

Someday, maybe my daughter will inherit it from me.

A Holy Man

Edward Feldman

In the cold, shadowed room that smelled faintly of incense and bleach, two masked men huddled over the dancing blue flame of the alcohol lamp.

"Spirit," whispered one and held out his hands.

The other poured a pale blue liquid over his splayed fingers.

Now came my turn. In a stiff, green cloth surgical gown and bleached white mask pulled tight under my eyes, I walked to Gopal, the chief Nepalese surgical tech, and held out my bare hands. I hoped whatever he was about to pour on my pampered white hands wouldn't burn the skin off my fingers.

"Spirit," Gopal said to reassure me. Gopal, a twenty-year-old with coal-black hair and an easy smile of yellowed teeth set in a face of smooth brown skin, stood a head taller than me, thin like most villagers, with eyes so dark above his mask that iris and pupil merged, indistinguishable. The blue liquid felt cool, then freezing, evaporating as would alcohol. I opened my eyes; my fingers, though blue, didn't burn.

The spirit was needed because the Nepal eye camp had no sterile surgical gloves. In fact, we had no electricity or clean water, few antibiotics—in fact not much of anything found in a modern operating room. The year was 1985, early stages of the World Health Organization's program to fight blindness in Nepal. I was the current foreign volunteer eye surgeon assigned to a remote village north of Pokhara, a lonely dot on the map of the West Himalayan foothills.

The first week of surgery had begun at the Nepal Blindness Project Eye Camp, and this eye surgeon, who descended from the sky from a place far away called Boston, felt conflicted, unsure what the hell he was accomplishing here.

My work in Nepal resulted from an impulsive, hasty decision. Two years earlier I had finished eye surgical training and taken a position at a major Boston teaching hospital. I treated private patients and dutifully manned the clinic each day in a repetitive sequence that began to lack meaning. Treating patients with the same itchy eye complaints and fighting defiant insurance companies had become a dull pattern that paid the bills and nothing more. I was the mule in harness, slowly turning the millstone in the same path, round and round.

Something was missing, perhaps some meaning in what I was living for. Did Boston need me, another eye doctor? Hell, if you closed your eyes and threw a rock in Boston you'd hit an eye doctor.

And then one night, a person I loved said something that struck like a blow to the chest, made me question how I was spending my life. She said, "Just think if your gravestone reads 'Ed Feldman, Eye Doctor.' And that's it. Nothing more."

This image rattled me, nagged for weeks until late one night I saw it—small print in an eye journal: "Volunteer for the Nepal Blindness Program." I sent in the forms and my curriculum vitae. The following month the acceptance letter and instructions arrived in a crumpled manila envelope.

I stuffed a duffel with clothes, dozens of Ramen Noodles, Quaker Oats granola bars, and vials of iodine tablets. I reported to the Infectious Disease Clinic, where I got punctured with multiple needles to prevent hepatitis, small pox, tetanus, and other nasty bugs. Soon I was jetting above the Arabian Sea en route to Nepal.

And now, extending my hands to be blessed and sterilized in the surgical theater of a remote mountain village, doubts gripped me by the throat.

The patient, quiet and still on the operating table, was completely draped in green cloth, but for the lone eye looking up to heaven. Villagers like him had walked miles of terraced mountain trails to the recently announced eye camp in the faint hope that the magic of Western medicine might cure their blindness.

Earlier that morning, as first pale light barely warmed the hospital gravel path, I had seen a son carrying his blind father on his back, the older man's limbs twisted and curled like branches, and a woman carrying a child wrapped tight in orange cloth against her chest. There were others. I don't know how long they walked, how many miles they traveled on bare bleeding feet, gray with dust.

I gazed through an ancient German Zeiss microscope. The huge dilated eye with the milky cataract was illuminated by flashlights held by two techs while Gopal, the tall and thin one, handed me surgical instruments.

"Westcott scissors and point-one-two forceps, please," I said, and for clarity made a cut motion with the fore and middle finger, as in the paper-rock-scissors game.

I cut into the tangled nest of conjunctiva membrane blood vessels. Instantly the blood oozed, as expected. I was about to ask for bipolar diathermy to cauterize when I suddenly remembered there was no electricity.

Gopal spoke Nepalese to Poori, the other tech. Moments later Poori handed Gopal an instrument that appeared to be a six-inch metal rod with a tiny ball on one end. Gopal thrust the ball end over the alcohol flame I'd noticed earlier.

Gopal quickly handed the metal wand to me. After applying pressure to contain the arterial bleeding, I peered through the microscope at the metal rod with its burnished metal ball. The ball was the size of a large pea with various sized blunt pegs sticking out, as though a tiny mediaeval knight had lost his mace.

"For blood," Gopal said.

Unsure at first, I soon figured out how to use it. The miniature hot poker would seal vessels, as they did in ancient times. In the few seconds that had passed, the tip had cooled too much. Gopal repeated the flaming, and images of the Spanish Inquisition flashed through my mind.

Once I got the hang of it, the device worked surprisingly well on the eye's covering membrane vessels, the conjunctiva, and the fascia. Gopal, though, had to flame it often. The patient felt nothing of the heated metal ball; though the camp lacked other medical supplies, it had buckets of two percent lidocaine anesthetic, which Gopal had previously injected to numb the eye.

The twin flashlight beams held by Poori and a nurse allowed just enough light to see the corneal junction through the microscope.

"Number nineteen round blade, please," I said softly. My throat tightened.

The ten-millimeter groove incision caused more micro-bleeding; the tiny, hot mace sizzled while clotting blood.

In the operating "theater," watching the American perform surgery, stood two eye techs and three interested villagers, all gowned and masked. Perhaps it was the village chief and his ministers of health checking me out.

"Left cornea scissors." I opened the wound right and left to expose the cataract. Then I placed the suture loop through the cornea so Gopal could retract the cornea with forceps and I could remove the cataract.

"Cryoprobe?" I asked.

Gopal's eyebrows rose in question.

"Ice ball," I said.

Gopal nodded and spoke to Poori, who took a special blunt probe to what I guessed was a tank of nitrous oxide. A loud swoosh exploded in the formerly quiet room, and the probe tip froze white, a lemon popsicle.

Gopal quickly handed me the ice white probe and reflected back the cornea from the wound to expose the cataract. I placed the probe ever so gently on the dense white cataract. It froze to the capsule, and I waited for a good ice ball adhesion.

Gently I rocked the cataract right and left to release the zonules, the tiny fiber connections holding the cataract in place. Then slowly, slowly, I extracted the opaque disc from the open eye, praying nothing else came out with it, uninvited guests such as vitreous gel or, God forbid, retina—the membrane of vision cells.

The audience heaved a collective soft "aaaah" as I handed the white cataract, still attached to the probe, to Poori behind me. I closed the wound with interrupted silk sutures and exhaled with relief.

The Nepal Blindness Program had no expensive ocular implants available for us in 1985. Those would come years later. After healing and suture removal, patients would get old fashioned Coke-bottle, cataract glasses that magnified eyes into an owl's stare. Cataract glasses were better than nothing, better than blindness. Formerly blind villagers could haul water, build a fire; a farmer might tend his rice again.

We did some nine operations then stopped for the usual prolonged midday meal. I wasn't hungry, but it was tradition, and this foreigner wasn't about to interfere.

I leaned against a cold concrete wall and watched the techs eat their daily and ubiquitous daahi bhaat, and more daahi bhaat. Yogurt and rice.

Gopal offered me a plate of bhaat with some sort of vegetable and ill-defined, stringy meat, possibly goat or some other mammal that he thought the strange visitor might enjoy.

"Danyabad, danyabad," (thank you) I said. "But no." I raised a blue-stained right hand.

Gopal looked puzzled. "Rothi?" he asked. "Bread?"

"No, Gopal."

The lines about his eyes wrinkled in wonder. He was bothered the American wasn't eating; the chief surgical tech had taken a personal interest in my well being. Then his eyebrows rose in a sudden burst of enlightenment.

"I know. Umaaleko paani," he stated as fact and smiled, triumphant. He stood and faced the kitchen.

"No . . . I'm fine. Just resting."

Gopal shook his head, but by now I knew that that didn't mean no. It took days to get used to that. I still didn't know about nodding. Nodding might mean yes, "who knows?" or something else.

When I'd first arrived, I refused to eat or drink anything local, having been sufficiently scared out of my mind by Bernie Wolfe, the infectious disease consultant at the Boston teaching hospital, who said I was going to die of a 7-foot parasitic worm that would make my intestine its condo. Wolfe told me to memorize one phrase: "Umaaleko paani"—boiled water. "It's a life or death," Wolfe repeated. "Each time they offer something, just say, 'Umaaleko paani'."

So for days, every time someone offered me an unknown food, I'd say, "Umaaleko paani"? The question I hoped they would understand: Was it clean enough for my weak foreign immune system? But I got numerous quizzical stares, as if to ask in return: Why is the American doctor so hung up on boiled water?

"You want rice, doctor?"

"No . . . umaaleko paani."

"Bread?"

"No . . . umaaleko paani."

"Tea?"

"Has it been umaaleko paani'd enough?"

I thought of a Nepalese person arriving at a Boston McDonalds, and when they ask "Cheeseburger?" he replies, "No, boiled water."

"Fries with that?"

"No, just boiled water."

I accepted the tea Gopal offered and sat watching the techs eat, pondering the source of an unsettled feeling, not quite nausea, more like waves in the pit of my stomach. Was it climate? The food? Time change? No, something else was hanging over me, a cloud that blocked the light.

What, I wondered, could volunteer American surgeons actually accomplish of any significance in Nepal? The land bled with poverty, disease, and too much blindness—cataracts, vitamin A deficiency, the scarred corneas of trachoma.

I remembered again the long line of villagers at sunrise each morning—barefoot, soot on their faces from indoor fires, the deep tuberculous coughs. Malnutrition and infectious disease ruled here. If you lived until you were fifty you were lucky. Infant mortality was extremely high. Life beat you down into the orange dust, and if you got up, it beat you down again. What could one accomplish in a single eye camp? A drop of compassion in an ocean of misery.

And yet most Nepalese seemed grateful; they smiled at you, their brown fingers pressed together to a point. Was it their religion that sustained them in this world, the promise of a better life to come, a reincarnation?

Conflict and guilt harassed me. Why? Many American surgeons had come to work in developing countries. They'd spend a week or two doing surgeries in remote jungle camps—usually India or Africa. With fancy cameras and zooming lenses, they'd take shots of a mother in rags, wide-eyed, begging with her baby. They'd document as though working for *National Geographic*, show everyone back in the U.S. a slide show, while the audience downed cheese and wine. What great humanitarians are we . . . a regular "Club Med Albert Schweitzer." Their photos might be shown in the local newspaper. "Dr. So-and-So helps needy in Africa." Enlarged pictures and testimonials would be hung on plush waiting-room walls.

I was to be in Nepal a mere three months, which hardly qualified me as a missionary doctor. Though the cataract surgeries were going well, I felt insecure in the O.R., as though balancing on a three-legged chair. I missed that high-tech stuff, my instruments and, yes, surgical gloves.

Was there truly such a thing as an unselfish act by a human? Or did we do good deeds for some denied, unspoken self-gain? Did Mother Teresa or Saint Francis have egos? Were they so charitable as to be spared thoughts about future rewards in Heaven? Did saints get jealous when another saint was considered more giving, more holy?

Nepal needed surgical equipment, antibiotics and modern hospitals—not visiting Western surgeons. Nepalese eye doctors were skilled and professional, as good as their Western colleagues; they needed money, not two-week charity visits by jet-setting orthopedic buccaneers and plastic surgeons; not foreign mucky-mucks coming and going.

In the clinic I had treated diseased eyes from trachoma, infants suffering vitamin A deficiency, and snow white cataracts in forty year olds with malnutrition. But what had I really accomplished?

Well, better than doing nothing, and restoring sight to a forty-year-old mother was not trivial. Nor was it medical theatrics.

Once home, I would omit the wine and cheese party, the "Disease and Poverty Sound and Light" show for everyone to applaud, then drive home in their BMWs and Volvos to their comfortable, heated Tudor houses in Newton and Brookline. Still, I had to admit, I felt no more altruistic than those who chose to stay home.

Black Monday

Jim Fitch

On Sunday, 7 December, I had just finished breakfast when the alarm for General Quarters sounded. I ran forward and up the ladders of the superstructure to my battle station in Flag Plot. As I tested my telephone headset, a marine orderly hurried in and clipped a radio dispatch to the admiral's message board. I picked it up and read the signal:

> TO: All Ships and Stations
> FROM: Commander-in-Chief, Pacific Fleet
> AIR RAID PEARL HARBOR. THIS IS NO DRILL. REPEAT
> THIS IS NO DRILL.

CINCPAC had run such exercises before, staging mock surprise attacks on Pearl, sometimes on Sunday. The dispatch had to be taken seriously, even if the story sounded familiar. The ship's catapults launched two of our four scouting seaplanes. They had been in the air only minutes when their pilots and radiomen became the first members of *Northampton's* crew to know the awful truth: This *really* was no drill.

A Zero fighter plane attacked them from above, guns blazing. Big red disks on the enemy wings confirmed a well-memorized silhouette. Dropping almost to the wave tops, the desperate American pilots made evasive turns while their radiomen/gunners returned fire. The high-performance fighter was out of its element so close to the ocean surface, and the mismatched dogfight ended abruptly when the Zero broke off and disappeared, trailing smoke.

Our aviators in outclassed old Curtis SOC-3 "Seagull" float planes had outflown Japan's hottest pursuit aircraft and fought it to a standoff with their puny .30-caliber machine guns, relics of World War I. When that news spread through the ship, an Aviation Ordnanceman who routinely serviced the seaplanes exulted, "Can you believe those guys? That took brains and balls!"

The rest of the day was total confusion. We had good reason to expect more air attacks and no way of knowing where the enemy carriers might be. Our formation steamed around at high speeds, waiting. Then came another radio dispatch from CINCPAC in Pearl:

ENEMY TRANSPORTS OFF BARBER'S POINT. ATTACK.

Barber's Point lies between Pearl Harbor and Nanakuli—where I had learned to body surf the hard way only a few months earlier. As it turned out, no enemy transports were anywhere near the Hawaiian Islands. No troop landings were included in the Japanese plan; it was strictly a hit-and-run mission. By Monday morning CINCPAC decided the enemy attack force had left the area, and ordered us into Pearl Harbor.

Black Monday

As the mountains of Oahu rose above the horizon, we could see towering columns of black smoke. A grey surface haze grew thicker as *Northampton* steamed cautiously into Pearl Harbor, passing one calamity after another. The wounded battleship *Nevada* had escaped from her mooring and almost made it into the open sea. She sat aground in shallow water where her luck ran out, dangerously close to blocking the channel. Astern of *Nevada*, off our port side, lay the focus of devastation. Battleship Row was a shambles.

Below the pall of smoke, a sticky layer of spilled fuel oil several inches thick had bled from gravely wounded hulls. In patches clinging to sunken ships the oil was still burning. Whaleboats and motor launches probed among the wrecks in a prolonged, futile search for survivors. Seagoing tugs and fireboats pressed in alongside crippled battleships, shooting high-pressure streams of seawater at stubborn pockets of flame.

Pearl Harbor was wrapped in an ungodly quiet. The routine working noises of a huge naval base were silenced. The ugly black membrane that choked the harbor surface muted nearly all the sounds of salvage efforts. I remember hearing only the burbling underwater exhausts of many small craft as they worked at picking up dead sailors.

Our home port, which only days earlier had throbbed with so much organized, purposeful activity, was numbed and helpless. I got the impression that nobody was in charge, and suspected most of those oil-smeared whaleboats and motor launches were operating without orders. Their coxswains probably took any crew they could throw together and operated on pure instinct, doing whatever seemed useful from one minute to the next. Even the firefighting tugs must be freelancing; they would not have waited for anybody at fleet headquarters to dispatch them.

Most of the battleships were moored alongside Ford Island in pairs. The outboard ships sat on the sea bed, their port sides torn out by torpedoes, their main decks nearly awash. Their inboard sisters, shielded from torpedoes, were still afloat, but ripped by bomb damage and seared by fire. The few crewmen we could see on the stricken ships moved around in trancelike slow motion, or stared at us listlessly.

Outboard of *Maryland* an unrecognizable hump of rusty hull plating and keel thrust up through the oil slick. The old battlewagon *Oklahoma* had rolled 135 degrees. Just a few weeks back I had spent a relaxed Sunday aboard that ship, visiting friends. At noon we ate fried chicken and drank warm lemonade at a mess table set up in one of the portside casemates, under the breech of a 5" broadside gun. That casemate was now upside down, its shined brightwork fittings and scrubbed deck crushed into the muddy bottom of Pearl Harbor. Rescue crews had rigged stages on the steep sides of the inverted slippery hull and were trying to open holes with cutting torches, to rescue crewmen trapped inside the darkened hulk.

Arizona's tall tripod foremast was pitched forward at a crazy angle, and the boxy foretop dangled high above the drowned void that was left where her forward magazines exploded.

Up and down the line of wrecked battleships, scrubbed paintwork and holystoned weather decks were fouled by oil and smoke stains or burned away. Familiar silhouettes were disfigured by ragged holes, buckled plates, and bent airplane cranes. Tangled knots of blocks and falls trailed from twisted boat davits. The stink of burned paint and the smell of bunker oil hung thick in the still air. The whole Pineapple Fleet, except for our returning task group, appeared to be dead or dying.

I stood paralyzed at the break of the forecastle deck alongside Wilson, Yeoman First Class, my boss in the Flag Office. After a long silence he turned to me and said in a husky voice, "My God! Fitch, do you realize it'll take *years* to win this war?"

My throat was too dry to answer. Wilson sounded like the voice of doom, but once he said "this war" he broke my trance. It was true—we were at war, whether one had been declared or not. I clung to one thought: This veteran sailor was assuring me were going to win, conceding only that it would take a long time.

Even before *Northampton* completed mooring to her usual buoy, the crew scrambled to get her seaworthy. A yard tanker came alongside and started pumping in bunker oil. Throughout the night a succession of lighters full of provisions and ammunition shuttled to our sides. Gunnery divisions replaced all target shells with service rounds and armor-piercing projectiles. The ship's boat and aircraft cranes covered all weather decks with stacks of powder canisters for the eight-inch battery, tons of five-inch AA rounds, and boxes of cartridges for the old-fashioned .50 caliber machine guns.

At some point during that long night, a fragment of a poem, title and author unknown, ran through my head:

> *For want of a nail the shoe is lost.*
> *For want of a shoe the horse is lost.*
> *For want of a horse the rider is lost.*

Yes, if that manila hawser had not parted while we were refueling, if that hawser had not wrapped *Northampton's* propeller shaft, if the Task Force had not waited for us . . . my ship likely would have been wrecked.

As bad as things looked, at least we had not lost any carriers. *Lexington* had been saved by starting her run out to Midway on 5 December. If *Enterprise* had been at her usual berth on the back side of Ford Island, she would have been destroyed. As it was, untouched *"Big E"* was ready for whatever was coming, and *Northampton* would be right there with her.

At first light on Tuesday, 9 December, we got underway again, part of a small task force on a high-speed run to Wake Island. Our column of warships moved smartly into the channel, heading seaward. Endless billows of dense black smoke still poured from Battleship Row and the collapsed hangars of the air station on Ford Island.

My first rush of shock had peaked. In that quiet dawn it gave way to a stubborn, numbing dread. Were we steaming out into the jaws of the combined fleets of Japan's Imperial Navy? The possibility did not seem at all remote.

The Charge Account

Georgia Fowler

"Honey, could you run down to Brophey's and get me a pound of ten-penny nails?" I was sitting at my grandfather's feet, making designs with the fragrant curls of pine falling from his plane.

"Alone, Grandpa?" We had made many trips to Brophey's together, but alone? Grandpa was trusting me to go by myself? "Yes, dear. You don't have to go around the block. Just run down the back way, and tell Old Man Brophey you want a pound of ten-penny nails. That would be a big help. I'm running out of time here."

Grandpa took his gold railway watch from the pocket of his shabby work vest, snapped it open, and looked at its face as if to emphasize the issue of time.

I scrambled to my feet, brushed away the pine curls that had clung to my plaid dress and long black stockings. I waited politely for Grandpa to give me the ten pennies.

"You can't get lost, dear, if you just run down the alley." Grandpa thought I was afraid. I thought of the time I had decided I could go to Piggly-Wiggly all by myself. Turning right instead of left when I'd finished playing at the fascinating turnstile, I had become hopelessly, sobbingly, lost. But that was before; before, when I had first come to live with Grandma and Grandpa, because Mama and Papa were getting a divorce. I was only four then. Now I was going on five. Of course I wasn't afraid.

"No, Grandpa, I'm just waiting for the money."

"You don't need money, dear. Just run down to Brophey's and tell Old Mr. Brophey that you want a pound of ten-penny nails. Just tell him they're for me. And please hurry, dear." Grandpa knew I liked to dally. He was usually so patient—if he was telling me to hurry, he must really mean it.

"Yes, Grandpa," I said doubtfully, then ran off. If Grandpa was in a hurry, what a waste for Mr. Brophey to have to send me all the way back for the ten pennies! I would just have to run all the faster.

Through Grandma's garden, I resisted the call of the roses beckoning me to stop for just one sniff of their wonderful fragrance; under the arbor, where Grandpa had made me a rope and board swing. I gave the swing a little push with my foot to set it in motion, promising to come back for a real swing after I'd taken Grandpa his nails. I pushed open the back gate, paused for a moment to look for a possible delivery van or vendor's wagon, then raced pell-mell down the alley.

At the back door of the hardware store, I stopped long enough to wipe my hands down the front of my dress before grasping the polished brass handle. I pulled open the heavy mahogany door. I pause to scan the store for the senior Mr. Brophey and listened to the soft swish of the door closing behind me.

I soon spotted Mr. Brophey across the store, talking with a customer. In an exaggerated hopping gait, I covered the distance and planted myself in front of him. I remembered my grandfather was in a hurry, but I also knew that children were to be seen and not heard. It worked. Mr. Brophey looked down at me and said, "Well, well! What will it be today?" Then, to his other customer: "This is Mr. Hill's little granddaughter."

Carefully, I repeated my grandfather's message. "My grandpa wants a pound of ten-penny nails. They're for him."

I didn't really expect to get the nails. In the first place, I didn't have the ten pennies. And now that I saw the bins of nails, I realized I had no idea what size I was supposed to get.

To my surprise, Mr. Brophey began to put some nails in the three-cornered galvanized scale that hung on a spring from the ceiling. I watched, hoping they were the right size, groping for words to explain that I didn't have the dime, but that Grandpa really needed the nails, and now. I was sure Mr. Brophey would say, "That will be ten cents, please."

But Mr. Brophey just handed me the small bag of nails, asked to be remembered to my grandfather, and returned to his other customer.

Amazed as I was, I remembered to hurry. After one of the young Mr. Bropheys let me out the back door, I ran up the alley, through the gate, under the grape arbor, past the rose garden, up the steps; I was breathless when I arrived.

Grandpa looked in the bag. "Good girl!" he said. Taking a nail from the bag, he began to hammer a board into place.

I watched a while, then played with the wood shavings I had found so fascinating only a short time ago. But the question wouldn't go away. Whether Grandpa was busy or not, I had to ask.

"Grandpa, how did Old Mr. Brophey give me the ten-penny nails, when you didn't give me the dime to pay for them?"

Grandpa laid down his hammer and grabbed a piece of sandpaper. As he sanded, he told me about charge accounts. "And so," Grandpa finished, "if anything is needed while I am at work, you could just charge it to my account."

"Oh."

My mind now free, I was able to find new pleasure in the shavings at Grandpa's feet. Soon the afternoon sun created a rainbow of color on the floor. Pouring through a high stained-glass window, it announced that it was time for Grandpa to pick up his tools, change clothes, and leave for his job. He was a guard for the Southern Pacific Railroad. The rest of the afternoon stretched out before me.

What to do? Sometimes Grandma told me wonderful stories about mad dogs or scary Indian attacks when she was little like me. But now she lay at one end of the divan, snoring softly. The calico cat was asleep at the other end. What to do? Pretty soon Sissy would come home from high school, but not until the big hand got to four. What to do?

Then I remembered the charge account. Ten pennies! Wow! I could get a three-scoop ice cream cone for ten pennies! One vanilla, one chocolate, and one pink. And I could do it myself! I looked at Grandma, still sleeping. So how could I tell her where I was going? I let myself out the front door and set off toward the confectionery shop around the corner.

I skipped along, singing: "With a skip and a hop to the candy shop, to get three scoops of ice cream."

Three scoops of ice cream! When I reached the shop, I wiped my hands carefully down the front of my dress, then pushed open the glass door with its beautiful golden lettering. I listened while the invisible bell announced my arrival. Mr. Abrue glanced up, then went on reading his *Oakland Tribune*. I came in almost daily to spend the penny I earned each day for sweeping the sidewalk. I usually spent several minutes in delightful indecision before the glass candy display case. Now, I walked directly to the ice cream counter. Mr. Abrue put down his paper.

"I'll have a three-scoop ice cream cone, with the chocolate on top, please." I thought Mr. Abrue might ask to see my ten pennies, but he immediately took the scoop from the glass of creamy water back of the counter.

"What do you want on the bottom?"

So it was all right! Breathlessly, I watched my cone grow. What a wonderful way to buy things! How come I never knew about this before?

Then, as Mr. Abrue held the cone out to me, he said, "That will be ten cents, please."

My shoulders sagged, but only for a second. I said, "Charge it to my grandpa, please."

"Isn't your grandfather Mr. Hill?"

Of course he was! If Mr. Abrue knew that, why didn't he give me the cone? I tried not to look scared as I said, "You know my Grandpa."

"But he doesn't have an account here. I'm sorry, Honey, but I can't give you this cone."

Horrified, I watched Mr. Abrue unmake my cone, returning each delicious scoop to its proper tub. What had gone wrong? A young man and his girl had entered the shop while Mr. Abrue was making my cone, and now they tittered in amusement. Feeling my face turn red, I backed out the door. The tinkle of the bell usually held such joy for me: now it only called attention to my shame.

Back home, Grandma noticed my quiet mood and tried to tease me out of it. Sissy offered to play Pollyanna, but I just pouted, waiting to talk to Grandpa. Time hung as drearily as laundry on a wet day. Finally, Grandpa came home. After dinner, he was ready to take up the carpentry project.

I stood for awhile, my hands behind my back, pushing the pine shavings about with my toe, searching for the right words. "Grandpa, tell me again how I got the nails with no money."

"You charged them to my account, dear. When you charge something to my account, it means I will pay the bill, so you don't need money."

"But Grandpa, it doesn't always work." My lower lip trembled.

"Do you mean Mr. Brophey wouldn't let you charge? Did Grandma send you to Brophey's?"

"No, Grandpa. Grandma was asleep. And I needed an ice cream cone. But Mr. Abrue wouldn't give it to me. An ice cream cone is ten pennies, just like the nails, Grandpa."

My grandfather frowned. "Well," I insisted, "it is ten pennies when you get three colors, Grandpa."

Grandpa laid down his tools and sat down on the back step. Taking me on his lap, he explained. "Honey, you can only charge things at Brophey's . . . well, at stores where I have a charge account. I don't have a charge account at the candy store."

"Will you get one, Grandpa?"

Grandpa was silent for a minute, stroking my hair with his big hand. "I don't think I could do that, dear," he finally said. "You might get something that isn't good for you. But you know you can always come to me and ask. If it is something that is right for you, then you can have it."

In the closeness of Grandpa's arms, the cone no longer mattered.

The Gasman

Chuck Kensler

Our tires crunch on the gravel as we pull up to a gas pump with a red Indian head sign above the glass bowl top. White paint has chipped and peeled off the walls of the broken-down station, but it doesn't look as bad as the junked cars, busted-up car parts, and rusted farm machinery scattered along the sides and back of the building. A car with a raised hood and a bent-down running board seems as if someone just quit working on it because there are a few tools left on a front fender. Cowboy music plays on a radio inside the station.

Dad slides out of the car, looks around, stretches, and yells, "Anyone here?"

"Sounds like Gene Autry might be," Mom says.

"Hey, anyone here?"

A long-legged man comes from around the back of the station. His greasy overalls have a broken shoulder strap and they're ripped at the knees. He walks toward us like he's important, probably because he's wearing an army cap with a red trim around the edge. A monkey wrench swings back and forth in his hand. His whiskers are spotted here and there like a mangy dog. He's got a bad eye . . . no color . . . white as a cloud.

"Wot the hell ya wont?" he asks. "Don't service no peckerwoods, Okies, or Injuns. We ain't got room in this-a-here town fer 'em kind. Bess they jis git on their way like them Gypsies do. Ya lookin Injun. Ya Injun?"

The gasman gawks at Dad while he pulls on his oily fingers and some of them pop. He knuckle-cracks one hand and then starts on the other one. He stares at Dad and smacks the wrench in his hand a couple of times, like he's getting ready to give something a good wallop.

"Ya ear me? Askin if ya Injun."

"Naw, I ain't no Injun," Dad says. "I'm just like you . . . a dim-witted, knuckle-dragging cretin."

266

"Oh . . . well ya still kinda lookin Injun," the gasman says. "No o-fense. Jis ain't needin hang-round-the-fort-buckskins settlin in this parts. Know wot I mean?"

"If I was Injun, wouldn't I be chippin arrowheads in front of my tipi on some highfalutin reservation?"

"That's fuckin fer shirr." The gasman moves the wrench from one hand to the other, looks at it, and moves it up and down like he's pounding on a nail. His arms have fat blue veins. One has a tattoo of a naked lady and there's an Indian arrow sticking into a red heart on the other one. He looks at Dad and says, "Ya ain't a colored . . . hair too straight. Then he looks right at me and says, "That kid's kinda dark, but ain't no woolly-head." He sees Mom in the front seat and asks, "That yur pruty white-lady wife with a white baby?" The gasman has slobber hanging under his lips.

"What's it to you, you slow-witted mooncalf?" Dad says. He must be mad at something because the vein in his forehead is sticking out like a Y in the road. I think Dad is mad enough to take off his belt and get after the gasman. Or give him a Dutch rub.

"See it's this a-way," the gasman says. "I wunder wot's a-wrong with wimmen that marry outside their color. Know wot I mean?"

Dad reaches into the back seat, grabs an apple, and sets it on top of the car. He opens his jackknife and puts it next to the apple. Dad loves apples. Sometimes he cuts long, curly peels off apples before he eats them. Sometimes he cuts open watermelons. Sometimes he cuts the rattlers off dead rattlesnakes, and if he cuts off its head, he buries it in a hole or puts a heavy rock on top of it.

I'm glad I'm in the car with Mom and Craig because the gasman sounds crabby. Besides my stomach doesn't feel so good. And my heart's thumping . . . *thump, thump, thump.*

Dad squints at the sky, then at the gasman, and says, "You talk big like you've gone to some kind of Jim Crow school."

"Ain't bin-a school. Hard knocks bin my school."

"Nothing wrong with that, cowboy."

The gasman doesn't look like a cowboy. He's wearing dirty work shoes, not cowboy boots, and he hasn't got a six-shooter. And I don't see his horse. Could be it's tied up out back.

"Oh, yeah, cowboy, I meant to ask if you've heard of Deadeye Dick? You remind me a lot of him. I hear he was good with a rope and gun."

"Nah. Never heared of 'im. But mightin be a cousin or somethin cause we got lots of Dicks in our family good with shootin."

"Tell you what, Mr. Dick. We found our way into this town, and we'll find our way out. We're here to get gas and use the torlet, not to harangue over your air-headed words. How about pumping us some gas?"

The gasman rubs his forehead with the back of his greasy hand, looks at Dad, and then at his wrench. His arm muscles are twisted tight. He stares at Dad. His bad eye looks like the glass-topped lid on a fancy coffeepot called a percolator.

Dad rubs the apple on his shirt to make it shiny. He holds it with both hands—like he's going to shoot a basketball—gets a tight grip, twists the apple in opposite directions, and the apple breaks in two. He takes a bite out of the juice-dripping half-apple. Dad puckers a sour-lipped smile and spits chunks of apple at the feet of the gasman, as if he's taken a bite out of a rotten muskmelon. Dad looks at Mom and points toward the station with his eyes and chin.

"Come on, Charles." Mom opens the door and says, "Come along . . . hurry."

Mom gets out of the car, stands with Craig in her arms in the shade of the station, near a skinny-ribbed dog that's asleep next to a stack of bald tires. I stand a bit behind her. I have shivery goose pimples. Mom bites her lip.

Dad picks up his jackknife and says, "You know, Deadeye, I could change your dirty way of thinking and disrespectful talk about womenfolk. See this blade? I call it the 'numbnuts' blade." Dad holds up his knife so the gasman can see it real good. "It has the power to change your way of thinking from 'ass' to 'grass' . . . quick-like . . . *zip-zip!* It'll change your voice, too."

The gasman stares at Dad for a long time with his good eye. He hunches his shoulders, lifts the wrench higher, and then steps back. He rubs his long scraggly sideburns, licks his lips, and then squeezes them closed. It doesn't look like he has any teeth or a chin.

"E m e r y . . ." Mom says, like she wants to talk to Dad.

The gasman tosses his wrench into a pile of broken fan belts, and then opens and closes his hand like he's got a charley horse in it instead of his leg. He gurgles and shakes like he might be cold, too.

Dad opens his mouth and wipes a corner of his lips with his thumb. "Know what, Deadeye? I've decided I'm not going to give you an ass full of leather, only because I don't believe in violence . . . except scalping. That's the hardest part . . . not scalping some poor son of a bitch after you've kicked him into next week. Understand?"

The gasman jerks around like a silly billy, works his mouth like he's got a chaw, nods, and says, "How much-a gas ya needin?"

Dad smiles, points his finger right at the gasman and says, "Now you've got your ducks right, cowboy. Fill'er up, check the oil, radiator water, and clean the bugs off the windshield. Oh, yeah, got a torlet . . . a flusher?"

The gasman points to the back of the station with his thumb, like the hitchhiker we saw a ways back. He starts pushing and pulling the pump handle back and forth, and I watch the gas get pumped into the barrel-shaped glass top. First, up to number 3, then it rises to 4, 5, and 6, and stops on 7. The gasman pulls back his cap, scratches at his long stringy yellow hair, and looks at the numbers. I wonder if he knows that Custer had long yellow hair.

Boy, do I love the smell of gasoline. Back in Fort Yates, there are gas pumps at the agency garage. One day, two big kids I didn't know asked if I wanted to smell the gas nozzles like they did, and I said, "Okay." We smelled the gas until a man in striped coveralls cussed and took out after us. He said he knew who our parents were. The kids yelled, "Gimp, gimp, with the wood-leg limp," and threw rocks at him. He about scared the pants off me, so I took off for home. But I still love the smell of gas.

Mom and Craig use the bathroom first. Then I go in, stand up close and aim straight, but when I turn to look at a drawing of a skull and crossbones on the wall behind me, I pee on the toilet seat, flush handle, and toilet paper. Dad goes in last while we wait in the car. The filling station radio plays, "... *Where trou-bles melt like lem-on drops, A-way a-bove the chim-ney tops ...*"

Pretty soon, Dad slides in behind the wheel, starts the car, and we drive away.

Out the back window, the gasman holds onto the gas pump handle ... like a puppet with a broken string.

The Belgian Congo, 1959

Rosemary Manchester

Early in the year the mission doctor passed through Jadotville on his annual tour of physical examinations for missionaries and their families. He updated the four children's inoculations, after I passed out homemade popsicles as good-behavior bribes. Then he turned to me.

"Go into the bedroom and take off your clothes," he said brusquely. "I'll be right with you."

The four children stared at him, heedless of their popsicles dripping onto the floor. I shooed them outside to play and followed instructions. I sat on the edge of the bed, lightheaded with embarrassment. He came into the room and closed the door. "Any complaints?" he asked.

I mentioned premenstrual cramps, occasional heavy bleeding. "The usual," I said, apologetically. "Nothing serious, I'm sure." He gestured for me to lie down. I stared at the ceiling while he inspected my vagina.

"Seems okay," he said, "but we'll be on the lookout for fibroid tumors." I didn't like the sound of that.

"Nothing to be concerned about," he assured me. "Just part of being a woman. Eve's curse and all that. I'll check your breasts. Felt any lumps?"

His impersonal hands moved across my breasts, searching for irregularities. He hesitated, his face intent, serious.

"What is it?" I asked, no longer able to endure the silence.

"Something, definitely something," he murmured. "Can't quite tell without a biopsy. Have to talk to your husband about this. Put your clothes on and we'll go over your options."

I trembled as I dressed and brushed my hair. Stewart and the doctor sat at the dining room table. Their conversation stopped when I joined them. Baba Samuel brought a tray of cups, saucers, Nescafe, milk and sugar, a steaming kettle. I spooned coffee crystals into the cups and poured in hot water, stirred in milk. The plastic cups and saucers were the colors of Campbell's soup, tomato, cream of celery, split pea. I looked past Stewart's shoulder, out the window where the children played on the swings. I could just hear their voices, not make out any words.

The doctor stirred his coffee, cleared his throat to get my attention.

"Well, you can fly down to Johannesburg to the government hospital, the best medical center in Africa, modern equipment, fine surgeons. Or I can perform the operation at the mission hospital up at Kapanga. I do this operation every day for the African women, and we send the tissue to Jo'burg for analysis."

He must have seen my look of dismay. "There's nothing to worry about, I'm sure. We've caught this in the early stages."

We sat in silence. Finally I asked Stewart what he thought we should do. It's up to you," he said. "What do *you* want to do?"

"I can tell you what I *don't* want to do, and that's go to Jo'burg. South Africa is the last place on earth I want to go, even if they have good hospitals. For white folks. I think I'd prefer to go to the States for this."

The doctor grimaced. "The Board of Missions would never approve that expense," he said, "even if you went by yourself." I looked at Stewart. He shook his head.

"Then I guess it's Kapanga," I said. I knew the doctor's reputation as a superb surgeon. If he thought he could handle it at his primitive hospital, I would put myself in his hands. I proposed that we take the children with us to Kapanga.

"Can't do it," Stewart said. "I can't take that much time away from the work. And I don't think it's a good idea to take the kids out of school just now."

"Linda Price needs to come up to the hospital, too," the doctor said. "She has some female trouble. The two of you could drive up together. A great opportunity for you to see the bush country." The two men seemed pleased to have solved the problem.

It seems incredible now that two white women could travel then, unescorted, for five hundred miles into the bush over primitive roads for three days. We prepared for every emergency, for fallen trees across the road, mud holes, flat tires. We made room in the little car for an axe, shovel, cables, gas can, tire pump, tire patches. There would be no gas stations after we passed Kolwezi. Neither of us knew anything about auto repair. We would depend on the kindness of strangers.

The rudimentary road that linked the industrial cities of the Katanga to the capital at Leopoldville was little more than parallel sandy tracks through tall grass and tall trees, where troops of monkeys chattered. If we met a car we would pull off into the grass, but all that first day we met only two cars. We traveled right through the center of dozens of villages and small towns, ramshackle mud houses with tin roofs or thatch, tumbledown roadside shops advertising Coca Cola. Flocks of frantic chickens and black goats ran into the road, and sometimes children, narrowly missed by our car. People ran out of their huts to cheer and wave at two white women passing through in a blue Volkswagen. We waved back, and I steered the car carefully down the dirt track, red dust flying behind us.

We had our instructions. If our car ran into an animal, or a person, we were not to stop. A dead chicken or goat would provide dinner for the villagers, but if we hit a person our lives might be forfeit. Linda and I talked it over; we had plenty of time to talk as we drove along, but we could not decide what we would do if faced with an emergency. Our compassionate natures weighed against our obligations to our children. We hoped we could avoid such a Draconian choice.

At lunchtime we stopped right in the road, spread our picnic blanket beside the car and ate our sardine sandwiches. The sun worked its way across the sky. Through the long afternoon we took turns at the wheel, driving through the monotonous landscape. We came to a river, unbridged. A toot of the horn and a no-frills ferry, boards placed across a dugout canoe, started toward us from the far side. Linda took the wheel and maneuvered the car along two narrow planks onto the platform. The ferry, attached to a cable, floated slowly across the river, propelled by the sluggish current.

We stopped for the night at Sandoa village. The missionaries there, alerted by the shortwave radio, were expecting us and had prepared the guest house. Gratefully we washed off the red road dust with warm water. The water was heated in a barrel over a charcoal fire in the yard and carried into the bathhouse by a servant. Dressed in clean clothes we joined the family for dinner, entertaining them with tales of our travels.

On our final day, as we approached our destination, we crossed another wide river on a perilous ferry. Halfway across we surprised a pod of hippos. They opened their enormous jaws and showed their formidable teeth, then sank back under the murky water until only their bulging eyes and piggy ears were visible.

At the mission we joined the doctor and his family at the dinner table. The doctor's wife was also a doctor. She limited her practice in order to have time for their young children, but she was fully responsible for the medical practice when her husband was away. Medical professionals seem to like to discuss their work at the dinner table, regardless of the queasiness of the guests, and the two doctors reviewed the events of the day, surgeries, injuries, accidents. Nevertheless, Linda and I relished the meal of antelope steak and hippo pot roast from a recent hunting trip, fresh vegetables from the garden, and pineapples that grew in abundance in the sandy soil.

Drums in the nearby village sounded through the night. In the morning we toured the overcrowded mission hospital at Kapanga, the only one for hundreds of miles, a rambling mud brick structure with a metal roof. A noisy generator provided electricity. No blood bank. No equipment for transfusions. A primitive laboratory. Two hundred beds, no sheets, no blankets, no mattresses; patients brought their own or wrapped themselves in whatever they had. Many slept on blankets on the floor. A recent epidemic had overwhelmed the hospital as many patients developed complications from bronchitis and pneumonia and malaria. Entire families brought their sick and camped nearby, prepared food over open fires for themselves and the patients, slept on the ground. The staff consisted of the two doctors; one European nurse, a woman; and a staff of African nurses, all men. I wondered if Jo'burg might have been a more prudent choice after all.

That Morning with Bea

Frank Sennello

"Good morning, honey," I said to my wife, Bea. "Here's your coffee."
I set the mug on her bedside table. She sat up and I moved her pillow against the wall so she could lean against it. She scooted back, picked up the mug, and took a sip.
"What day is it?" she asked. I told her and she added, "They're all the same, aren't they?"
"Remember my name?" I asked, hopefully.
She stared at me for a moment but didn't answer. "It's Joe," I teased. "She giggled. "No, it isn't."
"Is it Al? Irving? Wilhelm?" No reply. "Okay, then who am I?"
Silence.
"Am I your mother?"
"Noooo." Sometimes she thought so during the night.
"Your brother?"
"I have no brothers."
"Your father?"
"I don't think so."
"Your husband?"
"Maybe. I don't remember. But I know I like having you here, with me."
She finished her coffee, and I helped her stand up and put on the pink bathrobe she liked so much. "Oooh, nice and warm," she cooed. "You put this by the heater, didn't you?"
"Well, the house is a bit chilly this morning and I thought you'd like it this way."
She took my arm and we walked slowly down the hall to the kitchen. She liked that better than using her walker.

I seated her at the breakfast table and moved her tangram puzzle in front of her so she could work on it. It consisted of seven plastic pieces of different sizes and shapes that each day must be arranged into a different pattern outlined in the instruction pamphlet. Our friend Gene had thought of that. Might help; couldn't hurt.

As Bea worked on her puzzle, I scrambled some eggs, mixing in slices of precooked sausage. In the few minutes that took, she had the puzzle solved.

How can she do that? I wondered. Can't remember my name, but is a whiz at puzzles and games. Like cribbage. She says she can't remember how to play—and then beats me four games out of five.

I opened the blinds and sunlight flooded into the room. "And what would you like to do today?" I asked.

"I think I'd like . . ." She paused and furrowed her brow; her lips trembled. I recognized that tortured look and knew she was trying—and failing—to find the right words to answer my question. With her elbows on the table, she dropped her head into her open hands, covering her eyes. Her quivering shoulders told me she was quietly sobbing. I expected her to repeat that agonizing question: "What's happening to me?"

We finished breakfast and then lingered over our steaming mugs, coffee for me and hot chocolate for Bea. Then we headed back to the bathroom to wash and get dressed. I helped her out of her bathrobe and pajamas and turned on the shower.

"Oh, no, Frank!" she pleaded. "Don't make me do that. It scares me. I'm afraid I'll slip and fall." She always remembered my name when there was an emergency or when she needed something quickly. I liked that.

I turned off the shower and filled the wash basin with warm water. I washed her back with a face cloth and then told her, once again, how to wash the rest of her body. That done, I dried her back and we walked to the bedroom to get her dressed.

Well-practiced, I put her bra and panties on her with no problem. I had set out a pretty white blouse with red and green flowers on it, and a pair of slacks that matched. "You warmed these, too," she said. I helped her into those and buttoned the blouse. Next her socks and a newly purchased pair of black shoes with Velcro instead of laces. Bea couldn't bend over enough, so I put them on for her. "I like these," she said, as I pressed the Velcro in place.

Dressed now, she walked slowly over to her bed table. She put on her wedding ring and wrist watch. She could no longer tell time, but she liked wearing the watch and never forgot her wedding ring.

"What now?" she asked.

"Back to the bathroom to finish up."

She picked up one of those funny-looking combs women use, made a few swipes with it on her beautiful, glistening, silver hair, and smiled at me. "All done?"

"One more thing," I told her. "Now brush your teeth."

Her reply was a punch in the stomach. The breath was knocked out of me and my insides hurt. I doubled over in pain. Tears welled up in my eyes. I wanted to cry, but I couldn't.

Turning those big, beautiful eyes on me, eyes brimming with love and trust, she had asked, "How do I do that?"

Oh! Dear God! I had just lost another small part of my beloved Beatrice.

Blendon

Yvonne Wilcox

I remember Blendon, my grandmother's house in northwest England. I remember the firelight on the rich deep-red of my grandmother's Wilton carpet, the coal fire sending soft flashes of light over the Saturday-morning-polished brassware in the woolly light of a mild grey afternoon. The sitting room windows were crisscrossed diagonally with brown paper tape, giving a mullioned effect. This taping was supposed to reduce the chance of having the windows shattered by the concussion tremors of bombs falling close by. After, though, when the aerial bomb came down outside that window, the whole house moved, some of our apple trees were blown quite away, including the one with my swing in it, and not a window in the house survived.

But that was later. Today, we were sprawled on the carpet near the window, playing Monopoly. And it really was "we"—I was included, even though I was not yet four, and my sisters and cousins, all older. I could, after all, count properly, and I remember I bought a red place—The Strand, I think—and Charing Cross Station. But what I most remember is the feeling there—such a sense of belonging, beyond acceptance, of being part of that circle of family around the Monopoly board in that house, that village, and out into the familiar darkness of a blacked-out country.

Blacked out, because at night German planes would be sighted heading our way, and the air-raid siren would sound. Everyone would rush to the safest place they had, often the space under the stairs. There we would huddle, to the faint smell from the gas meter, until the all-clear sounded, sometimes hours later. Eventually my father and brothers built an air-raid shelter half-underground in our back lawn, and we would sit there, wrapped in grey blankets, wiggling our toes a hundred times to get our feet warm. I remember my brother letting me, at last, peep outside just for a moment, and I saw the gentle sprinkle of rain, and the Christmassy sparkle of antiaircraft tinsel.

Sometimes the air-raid siren would sound before my brothers were home, and they would have to take cover wherever they were, and wait until the all-clear to come home. And we'd wait too, and it's only now, years later, that I can realize the quality of my parents' vigil.

These should have been scary times for a child, yet I had no sense of danger. War was all I had ever known; for me nighttime was a time of interrupted sleep, of short hurried trips in the dark. We were bombed out many times. Once the end of my cot had to be taken apart to pull me out, after the cast-iron fireplace surround fell across it, followed by much of the ceiling. But I only said, "Leave me alone, I want to go to sleep." Ignorance sometimes is bliss.

Broken windows and minor damage could be boarded up, but if the roof were too badly hit, there would be a hurried decampment, to a church hall perhaps, leaving everything, until a new home could be found. I was the sixth and youngest child, so we needed quite a lot of space. But somehow meals were prepared and clothes were washed, dried and ironed. Somehow, the men of the families got to work in the early morning dark. There were no street lights, shop windows were unlit, buses had only very dim lights, and cars were rare. But in this world of shadows, life went on.

There was a oneness of effort in England, especially in those desperate years before the United States joined the war. Every scrap of paper, cloth, wood and metal was collected and reused. Bins were put out to collect feed for pigs—potato peelings, or the scant waste food from table or garden. Every family used these bins, which were emptied daily. Victory gardens were more than a hobby. For England, life's focus was clear. It was survival, and the family drew close.

I believe that I was privileged to grow up in a time where there was such clarity of purpose. Ironically, this was a harmony created by the madness of war itself, but as a child I could not see beyond my cocoon. And now, when firelight falls on my own red carpet, I am back at Blendon, and the name is like Peace on my tongue.

The Author's Favorite Quotes
on Writing

A first edition of his work is a rarity, but a second is rarer still. —Franklin
Pierce Adams

If you can't annoy somebody, there is little point in writing. —Kingsley Amis

*I think the whole glory of writing lies in the fact that it forces us out of ourselves
and into the lives of others.* —Sherwood Anderson

Talent is like a faucet; while it is open, one must write. —Jean Anouilh

Fame often makes a writer vain, but seldom makes him proud. —W. H.
Auden

*Reading maketh a full man, conference a ready man, and writing an exact
man.* —Francis Bacon

*Some books are to be tasted, others to be swallowed, and some few to be chewed
and digested.* —Francis Bacon

*At this time I had decided the only thing I was fit for was to be a writer, and
this notion rested solely on my suspicion that I would never be fit for real work,
and that writing didn't require any.* —Russell Baker

*Writers have two main problems. One is writer's block, when the words won't
come at all, and the other is logorrhea, when the words come so fast that they
can hardly get to the wastebasket in time.* —Cecilia Bartholomew

*At first the tendency when reading over one's prose is to find it perfectly lucid
and forceful, not to say sublime. This is because the mind that has framed it*

keeps on supplying its deficiencies from special knowledge and the memory of what was meant. –Jacques Barzun

When I am dead, I hope it may be said: "His sins were scarlet, but his books were read." –Hilaire Belloc

With a novelist, like a surgeon, you have to get a feeling that you've fallen into good hands—someone from whom you can accept the anesthetic with confidence. –Saul Bellow

It took me fifteen years to discover I had no talent for writing, but I couldn't give it up because by that time I was too famous. –Robert Benchley

Every writer, without exception, is a masochist, a sadist, a peeping Tom, an exhibitionist, a narcissist, an injustice collector, and a depressed person constantly haunted by fears of unproductivity. –Edmund Bergler

Any ordinary man can surround himself with two thousand books and thenceforward have at least one place in the world in which it is possible to be happy. –Augustine Birrell

Studying literature at Harvard is like learning about women at the Mayo Clinic. –Roy Blount, Jr.

A good heavy book holds you down. It's an anchor that keeps you from getting up and having another gin and tonic. –Roy Blount, Jr.

I have always imagined that Paradise will be a kind of library. –Jorge Luis Borges

For your born writer, nothing is so healing as the realization that he has come upon the right word. –Catherine Drinker Bowen

We are cups, constantly and quietly being filled. The trick is, knowing how to tip ourselves over and let the beautiful stuff out. —Ray Bradbury

As against having beautiful workshops, studies, etc., one writes best in a cellar on a rainy day. –Van Wyck Brooks

What is wrong with most writing is its flaccidity, its lack of pleasure in the manipulation of sounds and phrases. –Anthony Burgess

Nobody ever committed suicide while reading a good book, but many have while trying to write one. –Robert Byrne

It's important for writers to live first, to have something to write about. If you have enough to say, you'll say it all right. –Erskine Caldwell

There is only one trait that marks the writer. He is always watching. It's kind of a trick of mind and he is born with it. –Morley Callaghan

Finishing a book is just like you took a child out in the back yard and shot it. –Truman Capote

My point to young writers is to socialize. Don't just go up to a pine cabin all alone and brood. You reach that stage soon enough anyway. –Truman Capote

The discipline of the writer is to learn to be still and listen to what his subject has to tell him. –Rachel Carson

During the actual work of creation, the writer cuts himself off from all others and confronts his subject alone. He moves into a realm where he has never been before—perhaps where no one has ever been. It is a lonely place, and even a little frightening. –Rachel Carson

There are only two or three human stories, and they go on repeating themselves as fiercely as if they had never happened before. –Willa Cather

Every fine story must leave in the mind of the sensitive reader an intangible residuum of pleasure, a cadence, a quality of voice that is exclusively the writer's own, individual, unique. –Willa Cather

In my opinion, any novelist who can't lure a reader away from a bad soap opera is wasting his time. –John Cheever

The whole difference between construction and creation is exactly this: that a thing constructed can only be loved after it is constructed; but a thing created is loved before it exists. –Gilbert Keith Chesterton

Writing a book is an adventure. To begin with, it is a toy and an amusement. Then it becomes a mistress, then it becomes a master, then it becomes a tyrant. The last phase is that just as you are about to be reconciled to your servitude, you kill the monster, and fling him to the public. –Winston Churchill

Truth is shorter than fiction. –Irving Cohen

It's not a bad idea to get in the habit of writing down one's thoughts. It saves one having to bother anyone else with them. –Isabel Colegate

There are three difficulties in authorship: to write anything worth the publishing, to find honest men to publish it, and to get sensible men to read it. –Charles Caleb Colton

The Lord created Heaven and Earth and, as an immediate afterthought, writers. –Fred de Cordova

In Hollywood, writers are considered only the first drafts of human beings. –Frank Deford

Having to say something is a very different matter from having something to say. –John Dewey

What's so hard about the first sentence is that you're stuck with it. Everything else is going to flow out of that sentence. And by the time you've laid down the first two sentences, your options are all gone. –Joan Didion

Writing a book is like rearing children—willpower has very little to do with it. –Annie Dillard

A book of fiction was a bomb. It was a land mine you wanted to go off. You wanted it to blow your whole day. –Annie Dillard

Writing is turning one's worst moments into money. –J.P. Donleavy

Imagination is more important than knowledge. –Albert Einstein

Some editors are failed writers, but so are most writers. —T. S. Eliot

People do not deserve to have good writing, they are so pleased with the bad –Ralph Waldo Emerson

Nothing, not love, not greed, not passion or hatred, is stronger than a writer's need to change another writer's copy. —Arthur Evans

The tools I need for my trade are paper, tobacco, food, and a little whiskey. –William Faulkner

If a writer has to rob his mother, he will not hesitate; the "Ode on a Grecian Urn" is worth any number of old ladies. –William Faulkner

An author ought to write for the youth of his own generation, the critics of the next, and the schoolmasters of ever afterwards. –F. Scott Fitzgerald

Often I think writing is a sheer paring away of oneself, leaving always something thinner, barer, more meagre. –F. Scott Fitzgerald

A writer is a lot of people trying very hard to be one person. —F. Scott Fitzgerald

It is a delicious thing to write, to be no longer yourself but to move in an entire universe of your own creating. Today, for instance, as man and woman, both lover and mistress, I rode in a forest on autumn afternoon under the yellow leaves, and I was also the horses, the leaves, the wind, the words my people uttered, even the red sun that made them almost close their love-drowned eyes. When I brood over these marvelous pleasures I have enjoyed, I would be tempted to offer God a prayer of thanks if I knew he could hear me. Praised may he be for not creating me a cotton merchant, a vaudevillian, or a wit. –Gustave Flaubert

Follow the accident, fear the fixed plan—that is the rule. –John Fowles

A writer is rarely so well inspired as when he talks about himself. –Anatole France

Nothing gives an author so much pleasure as to find his works respectfully quoted by other learned authors. –Benjamin Franklin

No tears in the writer, no tears in the reader. No surprise for the writer, no surprise for the reader. –Robert Frost

Unprovided with original learning, unformed in the habits of thinking, unskilled in the arts of composition, I resolved to write a book. –Edward Gibbon

A unanimous chorus of praise is not an assurance of survival; authors who please everyone at once are quickly exhausted. –André Paul Guillaume Gide

Reading is a joy, but not an unalloyed joy. Books do not make life easier or more simple, but harder and more interesting. –Harry Golden

A detective digs around in the garbage of people's lives. A novelist invents people and then digs around in their garbage. –Joe Gores

For every book that survives the merciless judgment of time, there are nine hundred and ninety-nine rotting unread in libraries and nine thousand and ninety-nine that were never written in the first place. –Michael Harrington

When you've got a thing to say, Say it!/ Don't take half a day. Life is short—a fleeting vapor/ Don't you fill the whole blamed paper/ With a tale, which, at a pinch/ Could be cornered in an inch!/ Boil her down until she simmers/ polish her until she glimmers. –Joel Chandler Harris

The most essential gift for a writer is a built-in, shock-proof shit detector. –Ernest Hemingway

All modern literature comes from one book by Mark Twain called Huckleberry Finn. –Ernest Hemingway

A writer's problem does not change. It is always how to write truly and having found what is true, to project it in such a way that it becomes a part of the experience of the person who reads it. –Ernest Hemingway

For a true writer, each book should be a new beginning, where he tries again for something that is beyond attainment. He should always try for something that has never been done or that others have tried and failed. Then sometimes, with great luck, he will succeed. How simple the writing of literature would be if it were only necessary to write in another way what has been well written. It is because we have had such great writers in the past that a writer is driven far out past where he can go, out to where no one can help him. –Prose is architecture not interior decoration. –Ernest Hemingway

Literature: the art of saying a thing by saying something else just as good. –Elbert Hubbard

I'm not happy when I'm writing, but I'm more unhappy when I'm not. –Fannie Hurst

A student can win twelve letters at a university without learning how to write one. –Robert Maynard Hutchins

There's no thief like a bad book. –Italian proverb

Your manuscript is both good and original; but the part that is good is not original, and the part that is original is not good. –Samuel Johnson

I never desire to converse with a man who has written more than he has read.
—Samuel Johnson

If the book we are reading does not wake us, as with a fist hammering on the skull, then why do we read it? Such books as make us happy we could write ourselves. But what we must have are those books which come upon us like ill-fortune, and distress us deeply, like the death of one we love better than ourselves, like suicide. A book must be like an ice-axe to break the frozen sea inside us. —Franz Kafka

Literature is my Utopia. Here I am not disenfranchised. No barrier of the senses shuts me out from the sweet, gracious discourse of my book friends. They talk to me without embarrassment or awkwardness. –Helen Keller

You can write about anything, and if you write well enough, even the reader with no intrinsic interest in the subject will become involved. –Tracy Kidder

One of the really bad things you can do to your writing is to dress up the vocabulary, looking for long words because you're maybe a little bit ashamed of your short ones. –Stephen King

If you don't have the time to read, you don't have the time or the tools to write. –Stephen King

How can you write if you can't cry? –Ring Lardner

A good many young writers make the mistake of enclosing a stamped, self-addressed envelope, big enough for the manuscript to come back in. This is too much of a temptation to the editor. –Ring Lardner

Never argue with people who buy ink by the gallon. –Tommy Lasorda

Until I feared I would lose it, I never loved to read. One does not love breathing. –Harper Lee

When audiences come to see us authors lecture, it is largely in the hope that we'll be funnier to look at than to read. –Sinclair Lewis

Writing is just work—there's no secret. If you dictate or use a pen or type or write with your toes, it is still just work. I know that people want to hear about methods. They think, now if I knew exactly how that fellow or this fellow does it, I could do the same thing. –Sinclair Lewis

Every compulsion is put upon writers to become safe, polite, obedient, and sterile. In protest, I declined election to the National Institute of Arts and Letters some years ago, and now I must decline the Pulitzer Prize. –Sinclair Lewis

He can compress the most words into the smallest idea of any man I ever met. –Abraham Lincoln

Good communication is as stimulating as black coffee, and just as hard to sleep after. –Anne Morrow Lindbergh

All good writers are troublemakers, all good writers are sworn enemies of complacency and dogma. The storyteller's responsibility is not to be wise; the storyteller is the person who creates an atmosphere in which wisdom can reveal itself. –Barry Lopez

All books are either dreams or swords: You can cut, or you can drug, with words. –Amy Lowell

Every novelist has a novel in him, which is an excellent place for it. –Russell Lynes

If you think you're boring your audience, go slower not faster. –Gustav Mahler

I think it's bad to talk about one's present work, for it spoils something at the root of the creative act. It discharges the tension. –Norman Mailer

A writer is a person for whom writing is more difficult than it is for other people. –Thomas Mann

Literature exists for the sake of the people—to refresh the weary, to console the sad, to hearten the dull and downcast, to increase man's interest in the world, his joy of living, and his sympathy in all sorts of conditions of man. –M. T. Manton

In the novel you have room to make mistakes. In the short story there can be no mistakes—every sentence must count. –John P. Marquand

If you want to get rich from writing, write the sort of thing that's read by persons who move their lips when they're reading to themselves. –Don Marquis

Outside of a dog, a book is man's best friend. Inside of a dog it's too dark to read. —Groucho Marx

The first draft is a version without self-consciousness. –F. Van Wyck Mason

Only a mediocre writer is always at his best. –W. Somerset Maugham

A good style should show no sign of effort. What is written should seem like a happy accident. –W. Somerset Maugham

Get black on white. –Guy de Maupassant

Why writers write I do not know. As well as why a hen lays an egg or a cow stands patiently while a farmer burglarizes her. –H. L. Mencken

I'm a lousy writer; a helluva lot of people have got lousy taste. –Grace Metalious

In six pages I can't even say "hello." –James Michener

Writers would be warm, loyal, and otherwise terrific people—if only they'd stop writing. –Laura Miller, from a salon.com review of the movie *Finding Forrester*

Writing is the hardest way of earning a living, with the possible exception of wrestling alligators. –Olin Miller

As good almost kill a man as kill a good book: who kills a man kills a reasonable creature, God's image; but he who destroys a good book kills reason itself. –John Milton

Copy from one, it's plagiarism; copy from two, it's research. –Wilson Mizner

A book is the only place in which you can examine a fragile thought without breaking it, or explore an explosive idea without fear that it will go off in your face. It is one of the few havens remaining where a man's mind can get both provocation and privacy. –Edward P. Morgan

When you sell a man a book, you don't sell him just twelve ounces of paper and ink and glue. You sell him a whole new life. –Christopher Morley

First you're an unknown, then you write one book and you move up to obscurity. –Martin Myers

Everywhere I go I'm asked if I think the university stifles writers. My opinion is that they don't stifle enough of them. There's many a best seller that could have been prevented by a good teacher. –Flannery O'Connor

Ready-made phrases are the prefabricated strips of words that come crowding in when you do not want to take the trouble to think through what you are saying. They will construct your sentences for you—even think your thoughts for you—and at need they will perform the important service of partially concealing your meaning even from yourself. –George Orwell

Never use a metaphor, simile, or other figure of speech which you are used to seeing in print. Never use a long word when a short one will do. If it is possible to cut a word out, always cut it out. Never use the passive when you can use the active. Never use a foreign phrase, a scientific word, or a jargon word if you can think of an everyday English equivalent. –George Orwell

Asking a writer what he thinks about criticism is like asking a lamppost what it feels about dogs. –John Osborne

There isn't a story written that isn't about blood and money. People and their relationship to each other is the blood, the family. And how they live, the money of it. –Grace Paley

This novel is not to be tossed lightly aside, but to be hurled with great force. –Dorothy Parker

The last thing we decide in writing a book is what to put first. –Blaise Pascal

The first rule of style is to have something to say. The second rule of style is to control yourself when, by chance, you have two things to say; say first one, then the other, not both at the same time. –George Polya

Great literature is simply language charged with meaning to the utmost degree possible. –Ezra Pound

There is no reason why the same man should like the same book at 18 and at 48. –Ezra Pound

At last, an unprintable book that is fit to read. –Ezra Pound, on *Tropic of Cancer*

Masterpieces are no more than the shipwrecked flotsam of great minds. –Marcel Proust

We seem to live in a society that lacks communication. When you try to communicate, you're called a radical, a communist, dirty, a Republican, or something to let you know you're not speaking their language. —Richard Pryor

Put it before them briefly so they will read it, clearly so they will appreciate it, picturesquely so they will remember it, and, above all, accurately so they will be guided by its light. –Joseph Pulitzer

I read and walked for miles at night along the beach, writing bad blank verse and searching endlessly for someone wonderful who would step out of the darkness and change my life. It never crossed my mind that that person could be me. —Anna Quindlen

What no wife of a writer can ever understand is that a writer is working when he's staring out the window. –Burton Rascoe

I am sitting in the smallest room in the house. I have your review in front of me. Soon it will be behind me. –Max Reger

Writing is the only profession where no one considers you ridiculous if you earn no money. –Jules Renard

Literature is an occupation in which you have to keep proving your talent to people who have none. –Jules Renard

We all know that books burn—yet we have the greater knowledge that books cannot be killed by fire. People die, but books never die. No man and no force can abolish memory. –Franklin D. Roosevelt

The only reason for being a professional writer is that you can't help it. –Leo Rosten

My God! The English language is a form of communication. Conversation isn't just crossfire where you shoot and get shot at! Where you've got to duck for your life and aim to kill! Words aren't only bombs and bullets—no, they're little gifts, containing meanings. –Philip Roth

To turn events into ideas is the function of literature. –George Santayana

Every writer is a frustrated actor who recites his lines in the hidden auditorium of his skull. –Rod Serling

The true artist will let his wife starve, his children go barefoot, his mother drudge for a living at seventy, sooner than work at anything but his art. –George Bernard Shaw

My method is to take the utmost trouble to find the right thing to say, and then to say it with the utmost levity. –G.B. Shaw

The wastepaper basket is a writer's best friend. –Isaac Bashevis Singer

Literature is the memory of humanity. –Isaac Bashevis Singer

It takes the publishing industry so long to produce books, it's no wonder so many are posthumous. –Teressa Skelton

The skin of the man of letters is peculiarly sensitive to the bite of the critical mosquito; and he lives in a climate in which such mosquitoes swarm. He is seldom stabbed to the heart—he is often killed by pin-pricks. –Alexander Smith

What I like in a good author is not what he says, but what he whispers. –Logan Pearsall Smith

I used to be treated like an idiot; now I'm treated like an idiot savant. –Martin Cruz Smith, after *Gorky Park* became a best-seller

There's nothing to writing. All you do is sit down at a typewriter and open a vein. –Red Smith

A bad review is like baking a cake with all the best ingredients and having someone sit on it. –Danielle Steel

The profession of book-writing makes horse racing seem like a solid, stable business. –John Steinbeck

Write freely and as rapidly as possible and throw the whole thing on paper. Never correct or rewrite until the whole thing is down. Rewrite in process is usually found to be an excuse for not going on. –John Steinbeck

Writers are notorious for using any reason to keep from working; over-researching, retyping, going to meetings, waxing the floors—anything. –Gloria Steinem

A poet looks at the world as a man looks at a woman. –Wallace Stevens

There is but one art . . . to omit. If I knew how to omit I would ask no other knowledge. A man who knew how to omit would make an Iliad of a daily paper. –Robert Louis Stevenson

Omit needless words. Vigorous writing is concise. A sentence should contain no unnecessary words, a paragraph no unnecessary sentences, for the same reason that a drawing should have no unnecessary lines and a machine no unnecessary parts. —William Strunk, Jr.

They can't stop me. If people won't read what I write, that'll be too bad. If people won't publish what I write, I'll suffer. But they can't make me quit writing. They'll have to kill me first. —Jesse Stuart

A sentence should read as if its author, had he held a plough instead of a pen, could have drawn a furrow deep and straight to the end. —Henry David Thoreau

I put a piece of paper under my pillow, and when I could not sleep I wrote in the dark. —Henry David Thoreau

I have received no more than one or two letters in my life that were worth the postage. —Henry David Thoreau

With sixty staring me in the face, I have developed inflammation of the sentence structure and a definite hardening of the paragraphs. —James Thurber

My writing is based in truth, distorted for emphasis and amusement—but truth. It is reality twisted to the right into humor rather than to the left into tragedy. —James Thurber

Trouble in writing reflects troubled thinking, usually an incomplete grasp of the facts or their meaning. —Barbara Tuchman

To be a bestseller is not necessarily a measure of quality, but it is a measure of communication. —Barbara Tuchman

I didn't have time to write a short letter, so I wrote a long one instead. —Mark Twain

I conceive that the right way to write a story for boys is to write so that it will not only interest boys but strongly interest any man who has ever been a boy. That immensely enlarges the audience. —Mark Twain

Get your facts first, then you can distort them as you please. —Mark Twain

Most writers regard the truth as their most valuable possession, and therefore are most economical in its use. —Mark Twain

There are two weapons in the writer's arsenal. The first is stamina and the second is uncompromising belief in yourself. –Leon Uris

Failure is very difficult for a writer to bear, but very few can manage the shock of early success. –Maurice Valency

Temples fall, statues decay, mausoleums perish, eloquent phrases declaimed are forgotten, but good books are immortal. –William Vernon

The adjective is the enemy of the noun. –Voltaire

The art of writing is the art of applying the seat of the pants to the seat of the chair. –Mary Heaton Vorse

I love being a writer. What I can't stand is the paperwork. –Peter de Vries

When I see a paragraph shrinking under my eyes like a strip of bacon in a skillet, I know I'm on the right track. –Peter de Vries

I never can understand how two men can write a book together; to me that's like three people getting together to have a baby. –Evelyn Waugh

No passion in the world is equal to the passion to alter someone else's draft. –H. G. Wells

Once in seven years I burn all my sermons; for it is a shame if I cannot write better sermons now than I did seven years ago. –John Wesley

Writing is so difficult that I often feel that writers, having had their hell on earth, will escape all punishment hereafter. –Jessamyn West

Just how difficult it is to write biography can be reckoned by anybody who sits down and considers just how many people know the real truth about his or her love affairs. –Rebecca West

Advice to young writers who want to get ahead without any annoying delays: don't write about Man, write about a man. –E. B. White

The essayist is a self-liberated man, sustained by the childish belief that everything he thinks about, everything that happens to him, is of general interest. –E. B. White

I am beginning to feel a little more like an author now that I have had a book banned. The literary life, in this country, begins in jail. –E. B. White, in response to Army and Navy banning *One Man's Meat* in 1944

A writer is like a bean plant—he has his little day and then gets stringy. –E. B. White

The difference between literature and journalism is that journalism is unreadable and literature is not read. –Oscar Wilde

To write what you are interested in writing, and to succeed in getting editors to pay for it, is a feat that may require pretty close calculation and a good deal of ingenuity. –Edmund Wilson

I was always keenly aware that literature demands not only all one can give it but also all one can get other people to give it. –Edmund Wilson

I'm all in favor of keeping dangerous weapons out of the hands of fools. Let's start with typewriters –Frank Lloyd Wright

Writing is thinking on paper. –William Zinsser

Four basic premises of writing: clarity, brevity, simplicity, and humanity. –William Zinsser

Clutter is the disease of American writing. We are a society strangling in unnecessary words, circular constructions, pompous frills and meaningless jargon." –William Zinsser

There's no sentence that's too short in the eyes of God. –William Zinsser

Dear Contributor: Thank you for not sending us anything lately. It suits our present needs. –Note from publisher received by Snoopy in comic strip *Peanuts*

Writing is a lot like sex. At first you do it because you like it. Then you find yourself doing it for a few close friends and people you like. But if you're any good at all . . . you end up doing it for money. –Unknown

Glossary

Adjective. A word that describes a noun or noun phrase.

Writing is easy. All you do is stare at a blank sheet of paper until drops of blood form on your forehead. –Gene Fowler

Adverb. A word that modifies a verb, adjective, or other adverb.

Those who write clearly have readers, those who write obscurely have commentators. –Albert Camus

Alliteration. The use of words that begin with or contain the same letter or sound, in order to achieve a certain effect.

To eat is human . . . To digest divine. –Mark Twain

Antecedent. The word, phrase, or clause referred to by a pronoun.

I don't deserve this award, but I have arthritis and I don't deserve that either. –Jack Benny

Antonym. A word having an opposite meaning of another word. (See synonym)

♣ black, white

♣ up, down

♣ smile, frown

Appositive. A noun or phrase that defines the preceding word or concept.

Ronald Reagan, *the former President of the United States*, walked into the Oval Office.

My sister, *Della Street*, will arrive tomorrow.

Article. The word *a*, *an*, or *the*. Technically classified as adjectives.

Clause. A group of words that contains a subject and predicate. An independent clause expresses a complete thought and can stand alone. A dependent or subordinate clause does not express a complete thought, but rather depends on the main (independent) clause to complete its meaning.

♣ Two independent clauses: (1) *Marriage is a great institution*, (2) *but I'm not ready for an institution.* –Mae West

♣ Dependent/independent clauses: *If you want to look young and thin* (dependent), hang *around old fat people* (independent). –Jim Eason

Cliché. An expression, once fresh, that has become stale from overuse.

Avoid clichés like the plague.
Nice guys finish last, but we get to sleep in. –Evan Davis

Conjunction. A word that connects other words, phrases, and/or clauses.

♣ ridden hard *and* put away wet

♣ shaken *but* not stirred

Contraction. A word in which an apostrophe is used to indicate omitted letters or numbers.

♣ *don't* (for *do not*)

♣ *'20* (for *1920*)

Dangling modifier. A modifier that cannot logically modify any word in a sentence.

Running down the street, the house was on fire.

Gerund. A verb form that ends in *ing* and is used as a noun. (See Participle)

The art of living is more like wrestling than dancing. –Marcus Aurelius

Infinitive. *To* plus the present tense of a verb.

The power to tax is the power to destroy. –John Marshall

Interjection. A word or phrase that expresses strong feelings; an exclamation.

♣ Holy cow!

♣ Wow!

♣ How about that!

♣ Zowee!

Metaphor. The implied comparison of one thing to another, without using *like* or *as*.

A committee *is a cul-de-sac down which ideas are lured and then quietly strangled.* –Sir Barnett Cocks

Noun. A word that names things. Nouns can be classified as:

♣ proper nouns: Jane

♣ common nouns: girl

♣ collective nouns: bunch, herd

♣ pronouns: she, they

Concrete nouns refer to definite objects: *chair, apple, Janet*
Abstract nouns refer to ideas or concepts: *justice, liberty, destruction*

Participle. A form of a verb that either serves as an adjective or shows tense. Participles acting as adjectives end in *ing, en, d, ed,* or *t*.

♣ burning fire

♣ fixed race

♣ swollen thumb

Phrase. A part of a sentence that has no subject or predicate. [See Clause]

♣ Noun phrase: a city of fifty thousand people

♣ Prepositional phrase: above everyone else

♣ Gerund phrase: finding a needle in a haystack

Prefix. A word element added to the beginning of a root word. If, for example, you are against (anti) someone, you have an *antipathy* toward him; if you like him, you're in *sympathy* with (sym) him.

♣ overboard

♣ preregister

♣ postgraduate

♣ subbasement

Preposition. A part of speech that introduces a prepositional phrase. In the sentence, *"The cat sleeps on the sofa,"* the word *on* is a preposition, introducing the prepositional phrase *"on the sofa."*

Pronoun. A word that takes the place of a noun.

> *Every writer is a frustrated actor who recites his lines in the hidden auditorium of his skull.* –Rod Serling

Simile. A direct comparison using *like* or *as*.

> *A woman without a man is like a fish without a bicycle.* –Gloria Steinem

Split infinitive. A word or phrase placed between *to* and the verb. Although splitting an infinitive is not the faux pas it once was, skilled writers still avoid them whenever possible.

Split: *Applicants were asked to promptly complete the form.*

Improved: *Applicants were asked to complete the form promptly.*

Suffix. A word element added to the end of a root word.

suicide   forward   boredom   singing

Synonym. A word similar in meaning to another word. (See Antonym)

♣ giant/ huge

♣ insect, bug

♣ throw, toss

Verb. A word that indicates an action (to struggle), a happening (to occur), or a state of being (am, was).

To Help You Remember

Here's a little rhyme, by David B. Tower and Benjamin F. Tweed, which teachers
once used to help students learn parts of speech.

Three little words you often see
Are ARTICLES: a, an, and the.
A NOUN's the name of anything,
As: school or garden, toy, or swing.
ADJECTIVES tell the kind of noun,
As: great, small, pretty, white, or brown.
VERBS tell of something being done:
To read, write, count, sing, jump, or run.
How things are done the ADVERBS tell,
As: slowly, quickly, badly, well.
CONJUNCTIONS join the words together,
As: men and women, wind or weather.
The PREPOSITION stands before
A noun as: in or through a door.
The INTERJECTION shows surprise
As: Oh, how pretty! Ah! how wise!
The whole are called the PARTS of SPEECH,
Which reading, writing, speaking teach.

Resources

Suggested Reading

If you want to write memoir, read memoir. Here are ten quality works to prime the pump.

Pearl in the Storm: How I Found My Heart in the Middle of the Ocean
Tori M. McClure

Twenty Chickens for a Saddle: The Story of an African Childhood
Robyn Scott

Hands of My Father: A Hearing Boy, His Deaf Parents, and the Language of Love
Myron Uhlberg

The Beautiful Struggle: A Father, Two Sons, and an Unlikely Road to Manhood
Ta-Nehisi Coates

I'm Looking Through You: Growing Up Haunted
Jennifer Finney Boylan

Brother, I'm Dying
Edwidge Danticat

Heart in the Right Place: A Memoir
Carolyn Jourdan

A Long Way Gone: Memoirs of a Boy Soldier
Ishmael Beah

If I Am Missing or Dead: A Sister's Story of Love, Murder, and Liberation
Janine Latus

Dog Years: A Memoir
Mark Doty

Online Resources

Google the word "writer" and it'll bring up a mind-numbing 243 million websites. To get you started, here are a few quality sites.

Author's Site

memoirwritings.com
Valuable writing tips for the memoirists of all skill levels.

Finding an Agent

absolutewrite.com
Sign up for its e-newsletter and receive a free list of agents.

agentquery.com
A free, searchable database of agents.

agentresearch.com/agent_ver.html
Verify the record of an agent here.

firstwriter.com
Search through 750 literary agencies and 900 book publishers to find one that suits your work.

QueryTracker.net
Upload your query letters and agent experiences to help build a database of agents so you know what to expect when querying them.

writers.net/agents.html
Find an agent nearly anywhere in the world.

Getting Feedback from Writers

critiquegroups.com
Publishing news, agents, and signings. Members can form private groups to workshop their writing.

editred.com
Peer critiques, publishing tips, and ways to promote your writing and connect with publishers. The site offers a free personal webpage, and promotion/ marketing tools.

fanstory.com
Free contests and peer reviews. You can create your own contest and challenge other writers.

groups.yahoo.com/group/mikeswritingworkshop
Here you'll find a community of nearly 9,000 writers willing to share information and critique your work.

mywriterscircle.com
This forum boasts nearly 6,000 members and an active critique section. Also: a job board, a resource center, and writing games.

newbie-writers.com
A site for new writers. Subscribe to its free e-newsletter and receive an 85-page e-book resource guide.

oncewritten.com
For yet-to-be published or newly published authors. Offers original book reviews and book-giveaway contests.

internetwritingworkshop.org
Discussions and critiques delivered right to your e-mail inbox.

wordtrip.com
With 4,500 registered users, this site offers a forum to discuss all forms of writing.

writing.com
This site welcomes writers of all levels. Sign up and get a free online portfolio, numerous user tools, e-mail services and a chance to network with other writers.

Reference

brainyquote.com
Find famous quotes for your articles. Search by topic, author, or type.

dictionary.com
An Ask.com service with a dictionary, thesaurus, encyclopedia and translator.

m-w.com
Merriam-Webster's online dictionary and thesaurus, as well as word games, a spelling quiz, a Word of the Day, and the "Word for the Wise" podcast.

refdesk.com
Daily trivia that may lead you to a story idea.

chicagomanualofstyle.org
A site that offers affordable subscriptions to the most respected style manual. As they say, it's "the indispensable online reference for all who work with words."

wikipedia.org
The free encyclopedia that anyone can edit. It has short, interesting articles, news, and "did you know" and "on this day" features.

Acknowledgments

I'm indebted to the State of California, Santa Rosa Junior College, Joe Yull, and Betsy Roberts for funding, supporting, and supervising the Seniors Department and its Autobiography classes.

Special thanks to Chuck Kensler for both his riveting life stories and his incisive editing.

And to my daughter Madeleine, for her inspiration and her help creating my website, memoirwritings.com.

My greatest debt is to my wife Karen for the loving support that made the book possible, and the editorial and artistic talent that made it better.

Made in the USA
Lexington, KY
02 March 2012